FIRE YOU

Gain the Clarity You ...

Digital Marketing

Includes

30+ Printable worksheets to help you implement as you go!

Radhakrishnan KG

INDIA • SINGAPORE • MALAYSIA

Notion Press

No.8, 3rd Cross Street,
CIT Colony, Mylapore,
Chennai, Tamil Nadu 600004

First Published by Notion Press 2021
Copyright © Radhakrishnan KG 2021
All Rights Reserved.

ISBN 978-1-63633-772-2

Dedication

To my grandpa, who has always encouraged me to become the best version of myself.

To my friends and family for their respect for my work and relentless support.

To all my clients and customers whom I was fortunate enough to serve.

To the dozens of mentors who guided me in this incredible journey.

To my teammates who stood with me in times good and bad.

To you, for the commitment to up-level your business.

Table of Contents

Praise for the Book

This book is for everyone who wants to understand how digital marketing works. You don't need to be a digital marketing ninja to devise a successful marketing strategy. RK tackles far bigger challenges in this domain and that is - your fear that digital marketing is complicated. With mini exercises and step-by-step plans in this book, you are ready for the real game.

– Wioleta Burdzy Seth,
Co-Founder of Human Circle

Whether you're the founder of a startup or even a solopreneur like myself, this book is a very handy go-to guide on not just getting started in understanding what marketing is, but it almost hand-holds you throughout the whole digital marketing process itself. So you can walk yourself and your company right into profit. :-)

Having known Rk for a few years now as a dear friend, this book truly is a testament to both his experience as an entrepreneur and Founder of his own company, and his heart to serve his clients.

– Esther Isaiah,
Life Coach and Podcast Host of
'A Beautiful Conversation'

When I started my company in 2009, Digital Marketing was an option, now it is indispensable. I have known Rk for more than a decade now. His mission has always been to help business owners, entrepreneurs and professionals become better marketers. This book is a result of his proficiency in Digital Marketing and his passion for teaching.

Today, it is a world of inbound marketing - which is all about drawing customers to your doorstep. Becoming a thought leader in the domain you are in and pulling the right customers with the help of digital media is the game we must play to win. *Fire Your Agency* gives you a stepwise approach to thrive in your business by leveraging the power of digital marketing.

I recommend this book to my fellow entrepreneurs who are set out to meet their ambitious goals. This is a must-have handbook for business owners, digital marketing consultants and students alike.

– Vijith Sivadasan,
a Serial Entrepreneur and the Co-founder of Codelattice.

What I love about having worked closely with RK, and what comes shining through in this book, is his uniquely passionate and original style of breaking down complex marketing ideas and misnomers, to guide you right from building the right marketing strategies to detailing out the execution process step-by-step, so that you avoid the usual pitfalls and grow not just your business, but transform your mindset as well.

– Arun Varghese,
Product Owner at Practo Technologies

'Fire your Agency' is insightful and practical. It makes big, abstract ideas more concrete, by offering advice and complete action plans. This book will help leaders navigate a complex world of marketing with great insights.

I highly recommend this book to small business owners, entrepreneurs, startups and leaders.

– Shivani Gupta,
Founder of Macroskills

RK is a thorough gentleman and a successful entrepreneur who always brings to the table his core values, which include generosity. This is not a book you would want your competition to have!

Share more with the world, RK for you are indeed gifted!

– Pankaj Gupta,
Founder, The Pankaj Method®

Introduction

"Hi Rk, I need SEO for my website, how much does it cost?"

This is how most business owners approach me for help. They understand the power of inbound marketing and they want to capture as much traffic from search engines as they can. There's nothing wrong with this question, except they don't understand that they need an effective marketing engine that enables them to convert the traffic into sales opportunities, before driving traffic to the website.

It's like pouring fuel to a car that has a faulty engine that leaks fuel. Or like trying to fill a leaky bucket with water. Or like trying to catch a stream of water with a net. You got the idea.

It just doesn't work.

I have countless case studies on how I helped businesses generate 200% more leads from the same traffic they currently receive. We did that by optimizing their website and their funnels to capture the attention of the visitor and take them on a journey that leads to a predetermined conversion (registration, engagement, appointment, enquiry, or a sale).

Oftentimes, these were the same business owners who once thought that SEO would be the 'ultimate solution' to their marketing problems. But there are some critical factors that need to be taken care of, before we drive traffic into the website.

This book is intended for business owners who have aggressive growth goals, but are stuck between the realm of reality and aspirations. Business owners who want clarity on building their own marketing and sales processes before they delegate their digital marketing to an agency or their internal team.

"I've tried (Instagram) marketing, it doesn't work!"

– A Frustrated Business Owner

The worst thing about digital marketing these days is that there is too much information. Every "guru" out there is trying to sell "the next big thing", with tall claims that their solution is the ultimate cure to all the marketing problems. Business owners often fall prey to this scheme and when they don't see the desired results, they give up on it entirely without understanding that they need to get their basics right.

Also, I believe that startups and businesses does not need to hire an expensive marketing agency until they hit a high 7-figure or 8-figure annual revenues (in USD), since the founder-led businesses need to get "it" right before they have the clarity to delegate the high-growth activities to an agency. Till then, the principles in this book along with a combination of *Growth Recipes* and *Growth Ambassadors* are sufficient to guide them through the journey to hit these financial goals. You will learn more about it in the final chapter.

Hence the name of the book, FIRE YOUR AGENCY.

It is my sincere hope that this book helps entrepreneurs and business owners to get their basics right, get clarity building on their own unique marketing strategies and become ready to delegate the activities the right way, without being at the mercy of the marketing agencies that sell them heavy retainers and a huge advertising spend on top of that. Or worse, get taken for a ride by their own team who failed to show results because the business owner didn't know what to ask for.

This is the book I wish I had written a decade ago, to set the right expectations for our clients before beginning to work on their marketing. To enable them with the right mindset and principles to approach marketing the right way.

I hope that you enjoy reading the book and I implore you to take action along the way. Every chapter is accompanied with a collection of helpful Action Guides that you can download by visiting www.fireyour.agency/guide

Namaste,

Radhakrishnan KG

Chapter 1

· · · · · · · ·

The 5 Mistakes That Are Killing Your Marketing

You've downloaded several eBooks and courses, read and absorbed the tips, listened to the experts talk endlessly, and implemented everything you've learned. You've taken action but nothing seems to be happening, and you think you might have the beginnings of an ulcer.

You're doing all of the things you're "supposed to do," but you're not seeing results, and you're dangling over the cliff of burnout.

There's one simple reason why things aren't going right: you're making things too complicated for yourself. Sure, there are millions of strategies you can employ to let the world know about your business and its wonderful offerings. But that doesn't mean you should employ them all at once.

You're overwhelmed with too much information and shiny objects. You're multitasking yourself to death.

Instead, what successful business owners and marketers do is focus on one thing at a time. Once they get results from this single effort, they proceed to the next, having learned exactly what to do to get success.

Here are five reasons your marketing may not be working and what you can do to simplify for success.

1. You Don't Know What You Really Want

Naturally, any business has more than one goal at any given time. There are many different things you want to accomplish in different areas of your business, such as brand awareness, sales, product development, and so on.

But if you have too many goals at the time, it's nearly impossible to make significant progress on any one of them. You only have so much time, energy, and resources. They'll get used up quickly, and you won't see much in the way of progress.

Imagine that you're downloading an app on your smartphone. When you start downloading, you can watch your progress with the progress bar. One app takes maybe two minutes to download, but what if you download five at once? Chances are, you'll see that progress slow down, and in two minutes, you still won't have even one app downloaded.

To reach a goal, you need to break it down into actionable steps and sub-goals. One goal might break down into five or ten action steps. What if you have five goals simultaneously? Now you have 25 to 50 things to do. It's easy to see how difficult this would be.

The key for goal setting is not quantity but quality. Rather than trying to tackle everything at once and not getting anywhere, choose a specific goal to give your utmost attention.

Choose one goal that will bring you the best results in the shortest time. Choose the goal that's most necessary right now, or that you need to reach first before you start on another. Try to pick the one that will make the biggest impact on your business right now.

You need to prioritize and focus. This is how you achieve your goals.

2. You Don't Know What Will Work

You've learned many different strategies and now you're trying to employ them all at once, so you're all over the place. The better option is to choose one strategy that you know will work. But how do you know what will work?

Easy answer: You don't.

But marketing isn't about throwing things against the wall to see what sticks. It's scientific. Marketers try something out and monitor, learning through trial and error. If you're trying to do too many things at once, it's impossible to focus adequately on each strategy to see what is working.

The key is to take a good, calculated guess and choose a strategy you think will work. Then, implement it and monitor the results. What are the results telling you? How do you know if it's working? If you've chosen one clearly defined goal, this is easy to do.

A good way to do this is to work backwards. Start with the goal and ask yourself, "How will I know if I've reached my goal or not?" Choose metrics that are measurable. Set up milestones along the way that will tell you whether you're nearing your goal or not.

With a good goal, a good metric to measure, and milestones to help you chart your progress, you can implement your strategy and watch your progress.

For example, you want to build an email list. The idea is to create a list of 100 subscribers within a month's time. The strategy you've chosen is to create a page with a free download as an opt-in to get people to sign up, and drive traffic to this page for conversions.

At this point, you can decide that at the end of the first week, you should see 10 to 20 subscribers (it may be slow to start at first). At the end of the first week, check your metrics and see how many subscribers you have. If you have 10 to 20, you're doing well. If not, there's a problem and you need to examine further.

You might find that the traffic is coming but it's not converting. This means you need a better offer, a better website design, or something more relevant to offer. Make the appropriate changes, and start again. Then, measure your results and you'll know immediately whether the changes you made were the right ones.

Seasoned marketing pros do this over and over again and that's how they learn. After some time repeating this process, they know exactly how to design that page and exactly how to drive traffic to it. It becomes part of your marketing arsenal.

3. You're Suffering from Split-Personality Marketing

After reading the above, you might think you can handle running two or maybe three of these experiments with time to spare. But even if you have the time, energy, and resources to handle it, you shouldn't. Successful marketers don't do it this way. They focus on just one and see it through to the end, and this is important.

Marketers look for results and you don't get results without focus. Even if you have one goal and a number of great strategies for reaching that goal, you're better off working with one strategy at a time and giving it your full attention.

For example, something might go wrong during the course of your project that requires your immediate attention. With several strategies going on at once, it might be impossible to do this.

The key is that once you learn one strategy, you put it into your repertoire. Then you repeat it as you start on your next. You can delegate, outsource, and automate to make this more efficient. If you've repeated the process five times, you now have five activities going on that are completely manageable, and you know exactly how each one works. You're a pro at each of these strategies you have under your belt.

Scale this up, and you'll have a marketing empire.

4. You Don't Know What to Do Next

Once you've implemented a strategy and are monitoring its success, what do you do next? Do you wait around for it to reach your goal for you? No, that's probably not the way it's going to work.

A good marketing strategy is planned from beginning to end. The end is the final milestone where you can expect to have achieved the specific and clearly stated goal you made when you started out. Along the way, you'll have a series of smaller milestones to reach.

Each sub-goal or milestone should be broken down into concrete actionable steps. Think of these as the things you'd put on a to-do list. For a daily to-do list at home, you might list things like do laundry, call Mom, buy vegetables for dinner, etc. Each of these is clear and specific.

You can look at it and immediately know exactly what you need to do. The to-do list that comes from your marketing strategy milestones should be the same.

It's likely that you'll also need to deal with resources along the way. This means communicating to your human resources department, team members, staff, employees, or business partners who are essential to helping you reach your goal.

You'll also need to consider funding, technological tools, and other resources that you'll need. You should estimate what you'll need before you start so that you don't come up short once you get started. Try to overestimate just to be on the safe side.

5. You Don't Know When Something is Working

The way you know if your strategy is working or not is by monitoring it closely. But you'll face the same problems with monitoring as you faced with everything else: there are just too many options available and you can't monitor everything at once.

To say that the analytics software programs such as Google Analytics or Google Data Studio are "robust" with features, would be an understatement. These software programs are designed with the capability to monitor every single aspect of your business. You can have customized reports that detail everything, and it's tempting to take advantage of this.

But the key to success is to simplify, and just as multitasking doesn't get you closer to any of your goals, you can drown in a sea of too many metrics and kill your productivity.

Take whichever program you will use and examine its features. With your goal in mind, choose just a handful of metrics that will tell you clearly whether you're reaching your goal or not. Ignore the rest.

Not only is this approach more focused, it will also save you a great deal of time. You need to check your analytics on a regular basis and with just a few simple metrics to check, it's something you can do quickly.

The Virtues of Simplicity

Ironically, as the business world grows increasingly complex with new technologies and ways to connect, what we need to do most is simplify. This is true in other areas of life as well. Skilled marketers learned their skills by focusing on their efforts until they produced results, and then figuring out how to replicate and scale those results.

For now, don't worry about building a marketing empire. Start with the first step, and then move on to the next, and so on. This is how you learn the best way to reach your most important business goals. This book will set you up for success, like the launchpad to a rocket.

Chapter 2

* * * * * * * *

Success Mindset for Entrepreneurs

How to Cultivate an Entrepreneurial Mindset That
Inspires, Motivates, and Leads You to Success

*"My greatest challenge has been to change the mindset of
people. Mindsets play strange tricks on us. We see things
the way our minds have instructed our eyes to see."*

**– Muhammad Yunus,
A Social Entrepreneur**

Every small business owner and entrepreneur is in a relentless pursuit to grow their business. They usually do this by looking at external methods, such as outsourcing key tasks like accounting or installing automation software to take care of mundane tasks so they can focus on more important matters. They may try out new marketing tactics or sales strategies as well.

All of these external measures can make a tremendous difference in your business. But we often forget about internal factors, such as beliefs, attitudes, opinions, or habits of thinking, which have a massive impact on your business' success. In fact, these internal factors are instrumental in determining the success of your business.

What is Mindset?

In the simplest terms, your mindset is a collection of beliefs. It includes beliefs about basic qualities like intelligence, talents, and personality.

For example, you might have a certain view regarding your own intelligence. You may believe that you aren't 'smart' because you didn't perform well in school, as it's widely believed that school performance equals intelligence.

Or you may have a negative mindset about your talents. You may be asked to speak at an event that could lead to great opportunities for your business, but you decline because of a self-limiting belief. You may think, "I'm not a good public speaker."

Whether conscious or unconscious, these mindsets can directly impact your success. A positive mindset can help you activate your potential and reach heights of success you never imagined.

The Inner Critic

Your mindset and beliefs can be totally unconscious. It's not always easy to identify them, but that's what must be done in order to draw them out. For many people, a negative mindset manifests itself as an "inner critic." This is an inner voice or private conversation that occurs in your mind on continuous repeat mode behind your conscious thoughts.

Your inner critic tells you that you're wrong, you're bad at the task at hand, you're inadequate, or you lack the worth you see in other successful individuals. It acts as a judge, condemning you to failure at every turn.

Some people are aware of this inner critic while others aren't. Even if you're aware of this voice, you may be at a loss for how to deal with it. Many people believe that the inner critic is themselves talking. They mistakenly identify with it and this is why it's so good at sabotaging your life and thwarting your chances for success.

All of us have an inner critic. The first step to cultivating a mindset for success is to become aware of these negative thoughts and the impact they have on you. Once you've become aware of this inner voice, you've taken the first step toward releasing its grip on you.

The wonderful thing about mindset is that it's malleable. It can be developed or evolved. The negative mindset that's holding you back was shaped through experiences in the past and learned habits of thinking. Through even the smallest shifts in awareness or thinking habits, you can make profound differences, and eventually take control of your mindset and steer it toward positivity and success.

Learning Objectives:

By the time you complete this module, you'll be able to:

- ❑ Define and adopt a mindset for growth and success which will allow you to unlock your untapped potentials.

- ❑ Dispel limiting beliefs that you learned from school, work, or other negative experiences that are holding you back from achieving greater success and happiness.

- ❑ Identify and apply entrepreneurial mindsets and key ways of thinking that will enable you to do what you really want to do in your professional or personal life.

❑ Create a plan to further develop your mindset so that you can watch your business expand to new levels that you hadn't previously thought possible.

Action Steps:

Schedule 15-20 minutes today to do this exercise. Make sure it is during a time when you have no distractions. Close your eyes and imagine the type of life you'd love to have if anything were possible:

1. Does your ideal life include more vacations, more money, or better relationships? Write down the characteristics of your ideal life in the Action Guide provided.

2. For each characteristic, close your eyes and think about what each looks like for you. For example, if you have "financial freedom" as one characteristic, what does that actually mean for you? Does that mean having your house paid for by the time you are 45? Does that mean having your children's schooling paid for? Does that mean earning a six-figure salary? Write these down in the Action Guide.

3. As you are thinking about each of these, pay close attention to the thoughts that come. Are all your thoughts positive? These could be thoughts like "I've got a steady pipeline of new business, and my new marketing program is really doing great. It's totally feasible that I could make 20% more this year." Or are there other intrusive thoughts that pop up? These could be things like: "Yeah, right - a six-figure salary! Who do you think you are?"

4. Write all of your positive and negative thoughts inside the action guide. This exercise may take some time. Many people have trouble differentiating between the inner critic and their actual thoughts, so if you have not uncovered any inner critic thoughts, this may be the case for you. The key to this exercise is to become aware of your inner voice.

 Download the Action Guide:

Implement what you've learned, take action and start seeing results.

Visit www.fireyour.agency/guide to download the action guide for this chapter.

Reaching for Success:
Growth vs. Fixed Mindsets

Fixed Mindset

A fixed mindset means that you believe that your character, intelligence, and other abilities are static. This means that they are fixed parts of who you are and can never be changed.

A key characteristic of a fixed mindset is the need some people feel to constantly prove themselves. Since you only have a set amount of intelligence, personality, morality, and so on, you need to constantly prove yourself. People with fixed mindsets often get consumed in proving themselves in class, in their jobs, or in relationships.

This constant proving of yourself to others comes from the need to confirm your existing intelligence, talents, or abilities. This arises out of a concern over whether you will look smart or stupid, be accepted or rejected, succeed or fail. In this case, the individual with the fixed mindset is overly concerned with the static labels they have come to identify with themselves, such as "intelligent," "gifted," "talented," and so on.

Growth Mindset

A growth mindset is one where an individual sees character, intelligence, and abilities as always developing and evolving. Unlike the fixed mindset, a growth mindset doesn't compel you to constantly prove yourself because you know that you can change and grow with experience and practice. Your qualities aren't fixed. It doesn't matter if others see that you lack perfect qualities, because all of us are always growing and learning.

A key element in success in any field is the willingness and desire to learn new things and grow, and the acceptance of change. This is why a growth mindset is strongly associated with success.

Why Do Some People Have Fixed Mindsets?

A fixed mindset can be seen in a person who masters something quickly, and then plateaus and fails to improve further. The person will either succeed with a task at first try or give up in disappointment. Their inner voice has already told them that they're either good at or not good at the task at hand. A growth mindset can be seen in one who learns slowly and gradually, accepting new challenges and solving problems along the way.

Mindset Summary:

Refer to the table below to help you bring shifts in your mindset, from fixed to growth mindset.

Fixed	Growth
Intelligence, character, and abilities are static/inborn	Intelligence, character, and ability can be cultivated
Plateau early on, but may stagnate or not reach their full potential	Continuously reaching for higher levels of achievement
A hunger for approval; desire to maintain their status as intelligent; to have a good character; to have good abilities	A passion to learn and evolve
Effort in an endeavor is fruitless; it is better to stick with what you know	With effort, practice, and persistence comes mastery
Avoids challenges	Embraces challenges
Avoids situations where they might fail: Failure diminishes their sense of worth – the idea that they are smart or capable	Learns from failure; failure is an opportunity to stretch your abilities
Gives up easily when faced with an obstacle	Persists in the face of obstacles
Ignores criticism or negative feedback	Learns from feedback
Sees the success of others as threatening	Learns from the success of others

Adopting Your
New Entrepreneur Mindset

With this knowledge, you are now ready to look deeper into the entrepreneur mindset and start adopting the characteristics that will make the biggest impact on your success.

So far, in this course we've talked about both the "growth mindset" and the "entrepreneur mindset." The two are not interchangeable. Growth mindset refers to a broader kind of mindset whereas the entrepreneur mindset is more specific. However, the two share several common behaviors and characteristics:

1. **Positivity.** No matter what happens, an entrepreneur can frame it in a positive light. This is simply a matter of positioning or rephrasing. Instead of saying, "How can I avoid this situation?," an entrepreneur asks, "How can I correct this issue?"

2. **Learn from Failure.** Entrepreneurs generally don't achieve success on the first try. One of their key behaviors is that they try and try again. There are ups and downs and they're resilient and persistent. There will always be surprises and failures no matter how much you plan, and entrepreneurs learn from these failures and then move on.

3. It is easy to see how this relates to a growth mindset. When someone with a fixed mindset encounters a setback, they are likely to dismiss the task as impossible. They see it as a personal failing and give up in order to avoid further failure. An entrepreneur mindset allows you to uncover the lesson hidden in each setback or failure so that you can grow stronger and move on.

4. **Perseverance.** Just like the growth mindset, a key characteristic of the entrepreneur mindset is perseverance. Entrepreneurs tackle challenges head-on and don't beat themselves up over failures. They keep trying in a stubborn and dogged way, which is one reason people often mistake their genius for stupidity or insanity.

5. **Delegate to Others.** People with the entrepreneur mindset don't try to do everything themselves. They reach out for help and designate tasks for those who are best able to do them. Entrepreneurs are great at spotting talent.

6. Behind every great entrepreneur is an assistant or a team of executives and managers who handle tasks that either interfere with more important work or require skills that the entrepreneur lacks. An entrepreneur also recognizes their own skills and talents. They know that they should focus on planning their business and building relationships, not performing mundane tasks.

7. **Love of Learning.** The entrepreneur mindset loves to learn new things. Entrepreneurs have a hunger for knowledge and new ways of thinking. They embrace new technology, new ideas, and new theories. They

also embrace change, another key feature of the growth mindset.

8. **Intuitive.** Entrepreneurs are risk takers but these aren't just random risks taken for no reason at all. The reason an entrepreneur takes a risk is that they have a gut feeling it will work, or at the very least, teach them something valuable. As you raise your awareness about your limiting beliefs and mindsets, you'll also see an increase in your intuition and gut instincts.

9. **Follow-Through.** Entrepreneurs are always on the lookout for new opportunities even when there is not necessarily an immediate result. This is why they are good at following through. For example, someone with the entrepreneur mindset will follow up with everyone they meet at events, even if there seems to be no immediate benefit to doing so. They follow through because they know it could lead to something in the future.

10. **Flexible.** One thing that the entrepreneur and growth mindsets have in common is that they are flexible. They are open to continuous change and improvement, and they are ready to adapt or change plans at any given moment.

11. **Non-Conformist.** Entrepreneurs are not afraid to stand out and appear crazy to others. They embrace their uniqueness and they wear the qualities that make them different like badges with pride. One reason they do this is to differentiate themselves from competitors.

12. **Goal Setters.** People with the entrepreneur mindset set goals as a way to push themselves forward. The fixed mindset will tell you that a goal is impossible to

achieve or not worth striving for. If you're hearing this inner voice, reframe it so that you can look forward to attaining that goal.

13. **Good Company.** Finally, entrepreneurs surround themselves with other entrepreneurs, positive influences, and like-minded souls. They do this for networking, motivation, and to find mentors from whom they can learn.

As you went over the above qualities of the entrepreneur mindset, where did you find yourself? Did you feel that many of them applied to you? Could you see areas where you can change or improve?

Just as the growth mindset can be cultivated, the entrepreneur mindset can also be nurtured. In order to change your mindset, the steps are essentially the same.

Action Steps:

In Module 1, you wrote down ideas about your ideal life. Now, let's look at your business.

❑ **Write down some goals for your business.** They could be things like "grow my business in new markets"; "increase revenue by 20% by hiring sales-people"; "join an entrepreneur networking group"; "open a larger office."

❑ **Hear your inner dialogue:** Close your eyes and think through the goals you identified. List them. By now, you should have a good idea of where your limiting thoughts originated from. Write down the sources.

❑ **Reframe:** Reframe your thoughts using "growth" or "entrepreneur" mindsets.

❑ **Adopt your "entrepreneur mindset"**: Take action. You've now exposed your limiting thoughts, found their origin, and reframed them. Now write down any actions you need to take to continue developing different aspects of the "entrepreneur" mindset.

The Next Steps

Even a small shift to your mindset can affect a tremendous amount of change in your life. In this course, you have learned how to make these changes step by step. It all starts with identifying the limiting beliefs that are holding you back and transforming them into the beliefs of the growth mindset.

While you may have carried these beliefs with you throughout your lifetime, you can dispel them and make a positive change in your life in the time it takes you to reframe your thoughts and put your new beliefs into practice.

There are three fundamental steps that will make your new mindset take root:

1. **Awareness** – The negative thoughts that interfere with your success are often hidden just below the surface. These thoughts are in your mind, but they are NOT YOU. It is critical to understand this. We often identify with the negative inner critic and mistake it for ourselves.

2. **Reframing** – Once you know the inner thoughts that are stopping you, you can address them and turn them into something positive. An easy way to do this is to imagine that you're talking to a friend. When you imagine that you're talking to a friend, you'll naturally put a positive spin on what you say.

3. **Action** – Now, take the original action you wanted to perform before but that your inner voice was holding you back from. You're ready to take it on with a positive growth mindset.

It is incredibly easy to fall back into old mindsets. Your change won't happen overnight. Keep this course book and these steps handy, and review from time to time. Stay ever vigilant against limiting beliefs, which can try to come creeping back into your subconscious.

The growth mindset is a habit. Once you start turning your negative thoughts around, it will get increasingly natural to do.

Action Steps:

❑ Visit <u>www.fireyour.agency/guide</u> to download your Action Guide in each of the modules.

❑ List the steps you need to take next to complete the challenges you created for yourself for the growth and entrepreneur mindsets.

❑ Print out the graphic of the 3-step process (awareness, reframe, action) and put it someplace visible (in your office or on your desk). Refer to it anytime that voice creeps in and tries to hold you back.

Chapter 3

• • • • • • • •

Eliminate Business Overwhelm to Make Room for Growth

Prevent Stress and Avoid Burnout As You Increase Your Productivity and Efficiency

Overwhelm is one of the most common complaints among business owners and entrepreneurs. It can hit you at any stage, regardless of whether you're a start-up or a mature business. You'll recognize the feeling when you jump from project to project without completing anything. Or, it can hit you like paralysis, stopping you in your tracks before you even get started.

Feeling overwhelmed can wreak havoc on your business. If you let it continue without addressing it, not only will your business suffer, but so will you.

The good news is that you have the power to regain control and be the calm, efficient business person you know you're capable of. You just need to know the steps to conquering overwhelm.

This module will teach you how to eliminate overwhelm and reduce stress in your business. You'll learn the essential techniques and strategies to bring your overwhelm under control so you can once again breathe easily. You'll discover how to plan, prioritize, and manage your workload effectively, how to find more precious hours in your day, and how to return to a balanced life where you can see your family and friends more often. You'll find everything you need to take back control and eliminate overwhelm to become more productive and successful in future.

Learning Objectives:

By the time you complete this course, you'll be able to:

- ❑ Evaluate your current situation, so you are aware of what issues to address to bring about change

- ❑ Get all pending tasks out of your head and divide them into manageable chunks, so that you free up thinking space and retake control

- ❑ Apply a simple prioritization technique to your task list, so you ensure you get the important tasks dealt with first

- ❑ Reduce the size of your to-do list by eliminating or delegating tasks, so you can focus on the key tasks that will achieve your business goals

- ❑ Schedule your key tasks to reflect the time needed to complete them at your best energy times, so that you accurately plan their successful achievement

- ❑ Eliminate time wasters and drains on your energy, so you get the most out of every minute of the day

- ❑ Organize your work space and work tools to make the most of your time, so that you work efficiently on a day-to-day basis

- ❑ Avoid email overwhelm by implementing a system for managing your emails efficiently, so you don't waste time on emails anymore

❑ Avoid social media overwhelm by being proactive and disciplined, so you save time and get greater results from your social media connections

❑ Recognize the effects of stress and identify your own signs and symptoms of stress, so you know what you need to address to prevent detrimental long-term effects

❑ Establish a balanced lifestyle that suits your circumstances, so you can live a more composed, stress-free life

❑ Use techniques to reduce stress at an early stage before it becomes burnout, so you remain centered, calm, and healthy

❑ Consolidate and implement your learning and plan future action steps, so you can achieve the goals you set for this course.

The Three Keys to Conquering Business Overwhelm and Preventing Burnout

Are you feeling overwhelmed by all the things you have to do?

You might feel like each day brings a barrage of tasks that all need to be done right now. Nothing ever gets done and you're spiraling out of control.

If this describes you, you're not alone. Every entrepreneur or business owner feels this way at some point in their career. Even if you don't own your business, simply juggling work and personal life can be overwhelming.

Though it may seem hopeless right now, there's light at the end of the tunnel. You can learn to manage everything you need to do for your business and still have time to do what you love. It's all about taking control.

The first step to conquering overwhelm is to take a good, objective look at your daily activities and get organized so you can get ahead of the rush.

This does take some time and planning, but it's well worth it to increase your productivity and prevent burnout. There are several moving parts that can be reduced down to three pillars: Managing Yourself, Managing Others, and Managing Things.

Pillar One: Manage Yourself

The first step to clearing away overwhelm is to recognize that you are in control. It may not feel that way right now if you're struggling to keep up with all the demands coming at you from every direction. But the first step to conquering overwhelm is to admit that you have a problem and the power to fix it.

Put Tools and Systems in Place

Commit to putting in place tools and systems that will help streamline your business. Putting in the time to implement these tools upfront will save you time later on. There might be a learning curve, but it's all worth it when your daily life operates like a well-oiled machine.

Tools and systems might include software that helps you with scheduling or task management. It could be a routine for the start of each day that includes some light exercise and a few minutes prioritizing the day's activities. We'll get more into some of these ideas later.

Take Care of Yourself

The lack of balance in your life could be wrecking your health. Stress creeps up on us and can cause both mental and physical health problems.

Try a few methods to alleviate stress both at work and at home. At work, take regular breaks to get up and stretch, take a walk outside, make a coffee, or chat with a coworker. Allow yourself five minutes of mindless entertainment time when you need it.

On evenings and weekends, hit the gym, play music, watch movies, escape into a book – choose any activity that takes you out of your daily rush and leave work behind.

Pillar Two: Manage Others

It's not enough to just manage yourself. All of us have to deal with other people to some degree. Even if you don't work in a busy office, you might have clients, business partners, customers, and other people to deal with in the course of your workday. You can't control other people, but you can control how you deal with them to reduce your stress.

Set Boundaries

Set boundaries with other people. For example, establish a set working time when you're busy with projects. During this time, your colleagues or family members know to leave you alone. You might want to set break times where you're allowed to talk to others, but only for a set period of time.

Learn to stop overcommitting. It's natural to want to please everyone, but be aware of your capacity and don't go over it. Learning how to say "no" to people's requests is difficult, but it's crucial to managing your time effectively.

You can prevent overcommitting by padding your time and capacity to give yourself elbow room. For example, give deadlines an extra day or two. Let a client know why the job will take the time it takes.

Set Time Limits

If you find phone calls, meetings, and discussions often going on too long, set time limits for them. You can either do this explicitly by telling your colleagues a specific meeting length or just be mindful of the time and wrap up accordingly. For example, you can tell someone, "We have about thirty minutes for this phone call."

If a conversation requires more time that you don't have at the moment, schedule a follow-up, and jot down some quick notes on what still needs to be discussed.

Try to keep small talk at meetings to a minimum. It's important to open a meeting or discussion with some friendly chit-chat. You don't need to be abrupt, but once you get past the pleasantries, smoothly lead the discussion into the business at hand.

Pillar Three: Manage Things

Probably the easiest pillar to eliminating overwhelm is to take control of your physical environment. Making a few simple changes will make your work much more efficient.

Clear the Clutter

Looking for things you need under piles of junk can take up an annoying amount of your time. If you reduce the clutter and organize your workspace, you'll know exactly where everything is when you need it.

Here are some tips for eliminating clutter:

- ❑ Identify what you don't need. Get rid of it or store it in a place where it won't be in the way.

- ❑ Create an area for items you need daily. It should be within easy reach.

- ❑ Keep counters clean except for essential items.

❏ Stock up on shelves, baskets, and file folders and use them for storage.

❏ Keep personal and work-related items separate.

❏ Stay clutter-free by putting everything away as soon as you're done with it.

❏ Set aside some time each week for decluttering or getting rid of things.

You may find psychological benefits to reducing clutter as well. Many people feel that their workspace exerts a powerful influence on their mental state. A clean, well-organized desk can help you think more clearly.

Managing Time

Learning some new time management skills can have a positive impact on your work life and stress levels. You'll gain control over what you accomplish each day and how you handle all the things you need to do.

Start by conducting a time audit where you monitor how you actually spend your time. You can do this for both your work life and your personal life.

Using a pomodoro timer, you can time each of the activities you do throughout the day – checking emails, working on projects, attending meetings, phone calls, Social media, business planning, etc.

You may be surprised by the results of your audit. You might find that you're spending way too much time in meetings or on Facebook rather than working on long-term problems that could help to grow your business. Once you know where you're spending your time, you can make the necessary changes.

Time Management Techniques

There are many proven time management techniques that you can explore and implement. A simple but highly effective one is time boxing.

With timeboxing, you create a "box" for each activity with a set amount of time. How much time depends on the nature of the activity. For example, you might set 30 minutes for communications, one hour to work on an ongoing project, one hour for strategic planning, fifteen minutes for posting on social media, and so on.

You can take long-term projects or tasks and break them up into daily chunks. If you feel like you're spending too much time or not enough time each day on a particular activity, you can adjust the length of the box.

Learn to Prioritize

One of the primary ways to reduce stress is to prioritize efficiently. This involves creating a to-do list and ranking daily items in order of most to least important. For tasks that take more than one day, you can break them down into daily chunks. These chunks can be time boxes if they don't have natural stopping points.

Another approach to prioritizing is to assign levels of importance to different items. One level would be "urgent." Another might be "should be done." This gives you a bit more flexibility.

You could also list the hardest or most unpleasant tasks at the top. This way, you can get them done and out of the way during the early part of the day and then focus on tasks that are more enjoyable.

Automate Tasks

Take any tasks that can be automated and use tools to get them off your to-do list. Since a great deal of our work is now done online or using computers, things like scheduling can be done by a software program or app. Automation can really help clear up your schedule and take the stress off your plate.

Action Items:

1. What systems or tools would help you get better organized and feel ready to face each day?

2. Consider your work-life balance. Do you have clear times when you're off work?

3. How do you know when you're stressed? What stresses you? Identify a few activities that can help you de-stress.

4. What boundaries can you set that would allow you to better focus on your work without distractions?

5. Consider the strategies above for limiting time in meetings, phone calls, and other discussions.

6. Clear the clutter around your workspace and organize your space.

7. Conduct a time audit to see how you're actually using your time each day.

8. Try time boxing and explore other time management methods.

9. Develop a simple system for prioritizing each day's to-do list.

10. Brainstorm tasks you can automate and look for tools you can use.

Reduce Your To-Do List

Simplify Your List

How would you feel if you had total clarity about what you needed to focus on? If you knew that you were able to get everything done without stress? You'd undoubtedly feel lighter, more settled, and motivated to achieve more.

Look again at your business to-do list and see if you can simplify it further.

You may have noticed that there are tasks on your list that never get done, or tasks that have a consistently low priority.

There Are a Number of Possible Reasons for This:

❑ They could be tasks that can be eliminated altogether because they no longer make sense. They might have seemed suitable at one stage but don't suit your business anymore.

❑ Perhaps you have too many clients and can't service them all as you would like because your offers are too time-consuming.

❑ Maybe you have too many products and can't keep up with their progress or have time to create new ones.

❑ You might have projects that aren't getting you to your desired goals. If they aren't then they definitely need to be deleted.

These types of tasks are the ones that can really sap your energy. They affect your psychic RAM and take up precious brain space.

Make a decision about tasks you can cut from your list. Ask yourself, "Does it really need to be done?" If the answer is no, then delete it.

Plan to Delegate or Outsource

You may have tasks on your list that really do need to be done, but aren't.

There could be a variety of reasons for this, not just that you don't have the time. For example:

❑ You don't have the expertise or skills

❑ Someone else can do it faster

❑ It isn't a strategic task, so someone else can do it

❑ You know how to do it well but your time is better spent elsewhere.

If any of these resonate with you, then you need to delegate or outsource your tasks.

Look at the tasks and actions on your business master list and mark the ones that can be outsourced or delegated.

If you already have a team that helps you, see if any member has the time to take on more work and delegate the task to them. If you have a virtual assistant who works on general admin tasks, ask if they have the necessary skills.

If you have no one to delegate to, then you can outsource. If these are straightforward business tasks, then you shouldn't have any difficulty finding someone suitable to take the job on. If it's something highly specialized then you'd be surprised at the number of specialists you can find for hire online.

Don't forget your other to-do lists for home and family. There may be tasks on those lists that you can outsource to release time or energy so you can focus on your business. For example, house maintenance, cleaning, food delivery, and so on.

Finish Quick-To-Do Outstanding Tasks

All unfinished tasks take up mental energy. A part of your brain is still working away trying to complete the task, whether you are conscious of it or not.

You can't afford this when you need all your brain power to be your most productive self. These tasks could be on your home or family lists that you've been putting off while trying to focus on your business. When you're working on a project, you want to concentrate and not be distracted with thoughts of, "Did I get that done?" or "Do I need to do that?" or "Do I need to check up on this?"

Have another look at your lists. There might be quick tasks you can take action on immediately and cross off, e.g. a phone call you need to make, an email you need to send, an appointment you have to schedule, etc. These will generally be tasks you can complete in under 15 minutes.

Schedule time to deal with the tasks you have identified. Generally, a block of a couple of hours as a one-off will be enough. In the future, try to deal with these types of tasks right away so they never get on your to-do list in the first place.

Add Deadlines and Timeframes

The final step in creating an effective master list is to add timeframes and deadlines. Without this, you can't make the right decisions about how to allocate your time or other people's time. When you have deadlines, you can plan your time more effectively.

You need to set deadlines for yourself to make sure you achieve your tasks in a timely manner. And when you delegate and outsource, you need to give people a deadline so they know how long they have to complete the task.

A timeframe of, "This needs to be done by the end of the month or within the next 6 weeks" might be enough, but often a more specific, "I need this by 28th of the month" is more motivating.

Write down the deadline either in your diary or on your computer. You might want to set a reminder on your phone if you think you'll forget. There are also apps you can get to help manage your deadlines such as Alarm and Wunderlist.

Make sure your deadlines are achievable, as you don't want to put yourself or others under pressure. Don't set deadlines too far into the future so that you can keep some flexibility in your planning.

Action Steps:

- ☐ Visit www.fireyour.agency/guide to download your Action Guide.

- ☐ **Quick Win:** Look at your Business Master List. Identify any tasks on your list that never get done or that have a consistently low priority. Can you cut these from your list?

- ☐ Identify tasks to outsource or delegate. What actions do you need to take for which tasks?

- ☐ Identify any quick-to-do tasks. Plan time in your diary to complete them this week.

- ☐ Go back to your Business Master List. Take off anything you've identified can be cut. Then add in the timeframe for each task that's left. When you've completed each task, you can add in that date.

Chapter 4

• • • • • • • •

A Cure for the
Shiny Object Syndrome

Creating A Personal Development Plan That Leads
to Your Continuous Success

*"Learning is the beginning of wealth. Learning is the
beginning of health. Learning is the beginning of spirituality.
Searching and learning is where the miracle process all
begins."*

– Jim Rohn

One of the biggest challenges for online marketers,
entrepreneurs, and other small business owners is the need to
continuously learn new skills and concepts. In reality, most of
us crave the excitement of learning something new, especially
if it looks like it will help us in our business.

Challenge #1: Learning Addiction

The first problem comes when we let the exploration and
learning take over too much of our time. Or, even worse,
when we listen to something new even if it has no relevance
to what we're trying to achieve in our business right now.

Perhaps you've been lured by the excitement of the
Instagram craze. You can't resist listening and watching the

webinars about it. You've bought the latest course about how to use Instagram in your business, set up your account, and started posting. That's great if you have a very visual business and are in the middle of building up your social media marketing efforts.

However, what if you're in the middle of a campaign in which your focus is researching and developing a new product line? Does it really make sense to break that focus and take a detour to learn Instagram? Unless it's going to be integral to your new product line in some way, spending time on something unrelated will just slow you down in getting your product to market. No new product means less revenue.

On the other hand, what if you've already created your new product line and are looking for ways to get it in front of potential customers' eyes? Instagram could very well be a great place to achieve that. If you decide that your market is there on Instagram in a big way, then investing the time and money in all those webinars and ebooks may be just what you need to get new sales.

Challenge #2: All Talk and No Action

The other challenge we encounter with learning is actually putting it into action. Many times we pick up a great course or training program that we know will help our business. We start reading it and implementing some of it with gusto. After a while, though, it starts getting shoved aside for "tomorrow" as more and more daily tasks get in the way. Soon, it's relegated to a corner of the desk and then the bookshelf or a forgotten folder on the computer, gathering dust.

Successful entrepreneurs manage to overcome both of these challenges in a number of ways. There is no secret recipe for their success, but they do follow a few specific guidelines. Follow these and you'll be able to achieve the results you desire for yourself:

- ❑ Focus only on what's relevant to your goals Right Now

- ❑ Be specific about what you want to learn and why

- ❑ Finish what you started before you begin learning something new

- ❑ Apply everything you learn to real life, whether it's work or personal

Let these principles guide you whenever you feel the urge to embark on a new course of learning. Post them on your wall if you have to. Remember that everyone else is facing these same challenges and you are absolutely capable of overcoming them. Put all your learning to work for you so that you can achieve the success you've set your sights on.

In this report, you're going to learn how to avoid and conquer your two main learning challenges. By the time you're done reading, you'll be able to:

- ❑ Avoid learning about skills and concepts that aren't relevant to your business right now

- ❑ Pick out what IS important for your business and your own development needs

- ❑ Follow through and complete the course, book, program or other training that you've picked out

- ❑ Implement what you have learned so that it increases your business success

We're going to cover 10 critical steps for achieving these learning goals:

1. Establish a Mindset for Success

2. Figure Out What You Need to Know

3. Prioritize Your Learning Needs

4. Take Stock and Create a Resource Inventory

5. Choose the Right Training Program

6. Set Objectives Before You Start Learning

7. Limit Your Learning Time

8. Hold Yourself Accountable and Get It Done

9. Motivate Yourself by Measuring Success

10. Get Back on Track When You Wander Off

You'll get tips for implementing each of these, along with an Action Guide to help you plan how you'll take action. Happy learning!

Establish a Mindset for Success

"Wisdom without education is like silver in the mine."

– Benjamin Franklin

A chieving success at anything you do is far simpler than you think. The key is to be a good learner. If you study any successful entrepreneur, you'll find that they don't necessarily have superhuman talents. What they do have is the determination to use all of their life experiences to learn from. Then they take that learning and apply it to whatever they're working on at the moment. And they never stop learning, even after they have attained their dreams.

Being a successful learner is all about being open, paying attention to everything around you, and putting what you learn into action. Sound easy? It certainly isn't easy for everyone. Here are some of the most common barriers to learning success that may be holding you back.

No Clear Plan

If your learning goals aren't clear, you'll lose your way quickly. You can't get where you're going if you don't know where that is. Start by writing down a goal for what you want to learn and why. Be as specific as possible. Make sure that your written goal can be measured somehow. This way, you'll know when you've reached it. With this goal in mind, you can also brainstorm ideas for steps to help you get there.

Too Much at Once

It's exhausting and futile to learn anything when you're spreading yourself too thin. While there's a lot to learn on any given subject, you can't take it in all at once. Learning works in stages. You start with something basic, then add another layer, move to the next, and so on. If you haven't completed one stage, you won't be ready for the next. Focus on learning just one thing at a time. Once it's fully worked into your routine and you're comfortable with it, you can start adding more complexity.

Distractions

Distractions are everywhere, especially on the Internet. In order to learn something new, you need a clear focus. It's tough to shut out all the noise but there are some ways to effectively reduce it. One is to establish working time, learning time, and non-working time.

During your working time, ask yourself of everything you do, 'how is this getting me closer to my business goals?' If it's not, save it for one of your other time slots. During your learning time, ask yourself, 'how is this getting me closer to my learning goals?' Not relevant? Put it in your non-working or working slots. During your non-working time, indulge in all of your distractions to your heart's content.

Fear of Failure

You may be scared to act because you're afraid your efforts will fail, but this is the biggest barrier to learning. You must realize that failure teaches us the best lessons. You fail, you survive it, and you take away from it a valuable lesson. These are the 'hard knocks' that teach you through experience. In fact, to really cultivate the success mindset, erase the word 'failure' from your vocabulary. Replace it with the word 'lesson.'

Fear of Success

Strangely enough, it may be fear of success that's holding you back. This comes from a deep-seated belief that you don't deserve success. You feel like, 'it's not me.' The truth is that if you work hard, you deserve the fruits of your labor. As you work your way toward your goals, you'll become more comfortable seeing yourself as the successful person you want to be.

Know You're Going to Make It

Adopting the success mindset doesn't involve taking on anything new; it involves losing the things that are holding you back. As you identify these barriers and remove them, go forward knowing that you're going to be successful. This self-confidence is what's going to help you beat all the obstacles that stand in your way. Not feeling self-confident? Fake it! Sometimes just pretending to act a certain way makes it become reality.

Action Steps:

☐ Write down your goals for learning in positive statements.

☐ Eg: "I will learn to create videos from PowerPoint slides and use them to teach my customers how to use my products".

Set Objectives Before You Start Learning

"Setting goals is the first step in turning the invisible into the visible."

– Tony Robbins

The most effective learning happens when you set goals for yourself. Whether you're attending a conference, taking an online course, reading an eBook or doing an online class, having clear goals in your mind helps you filter out content that's irrelevant. Instead, you can focus on all the parts that will help you meet your ultimate objective.

Limit It to One

You might have a lot of different reasons for taking a course. It may offer benefits in different areas of your life. However, we learn best when we narrow it down to just one. Otherwise, you're trying to do everything at once and not getting any one thing done well. You'll get distracted and overwhelmed. Take all of your reasons for studying the course and narrow them down to just the one that's most important. Ask yourself: If you take just one thing away from this course, what will it be?

Make Your Objective Specific

When you take a course and learn something new, you want to integrate it with your life. So, your objective should be related directly to your business or your life. For example, taking a weight loss course because you want to lose weight is an adequate objective; but an even better one is to take the course so that you can impress people at your high school reunion. If you're learning HTML, your objective might be to improve your computer skills and understanding of the Internet. But a far better one is to learn it so you can create a website for your business.

Post Your Goal Everywhere

Take your objective and post it everywhere possible. Write it down and hang it above your computer so it's always visible. Carry it around on a little piece of paper. Tell all of your friends on Facebook about it and blog about it. The more you put words to your goal, the more real it becomes to you. Plus, the more you tell people about it, the more you feel like you have to follow through.

Set Your Schedule

No goal ever gets done without a deadline. Choose a date for finishing the course. Then, work backwards from that date and break the course into chunks. For example, if you've got eight videos in a training program to get through and you decide you want it done in one month, that's two sections a week. You can always change the date slightly if it's too much or too little, but don't make a habit of pushing aside your learning time. And don't forget to allow time for exercises and other components of the course.

Get Exactly What You Need from It

Here's a story that'll blow you away. You probably know that there are $10,000+ seminars offered by big-name gurus offline. You know that if you pay that much to attend, you're going to get the most out of the program. Well, there are some attendees who leave in the middle and they're the best students.

Why is that? It's because they learned exactly what they needed to know. Their learning objective was met halfway through the course, so why bother with the rest? Anything more would have distracted them from the reason they were there. It sounds crazy, but it illustrates an important point. For best results, let your objective guide you in your learning. Don't bother with anything that doesn't help you meet that objective.

Hold Yourself Accountable and Get It Done

"What you have to do and the way you have to do it is incredibly simple. Whether you are willing to do it, that's another matter."

– Peter F. Drucker

When you're learning something new, taking initial action and starting to put it to use is the easiest part. What's truly difficult is finishing the course and following through on what you learned. In order to get all the way through the important parts of a course, you need to be accountable. This means that you need to firmly hold yourself to your goal of getting it done.

Accountability Partners

One of the best ways to hold yourself accountable is to get an accountability partner. If you tell someone what you're going to do, it makes you much less likely to quit in the middle. You tell them your plan and they help to keep you on track. They do their job just by listening to you. You can do the same thing in return for them. There's nothing else an accountability partner really needs to do, other than to check in on a regular basis to discuss your progress.

Choosing an Accountability Partner

Your accountability partner can be a friend, coach, mentor, spouse, colleague, family member... just about anybody. It doesn't matter who the person is, but it should be someone who has a positive influence on you. They should believe that you're going to follow through on your promise.

It's a good idea to ask a third party that's uninvolved in the process and has no vested interest. If they're acting in their own interests, they won't be able to offer you the unconditional support that you need. It's not really such a huge responsibility; they mostly need to just be there to listen.

How to Use Your Acquaintances as Accountability Partners

There's a great way to use everyone you know as de facto accountability partners. Announce your plans and chart your progress on social media sites like Facebook and Twitter. You'll have a really hard time giving up when you know that you have to announce it to your 250+ friends and followers! You'll stay on track just to avoid the comments it'll draw.

Join a Group

You can also join a group of people in the same boat as you. There are online groups and forums with every interest under the sun. Find one related to what you're doing and join. Then, introduce yourself to the group and tell them what you're doing. You'll find plenty of support in a good forum, as well as tips on how to learn.

Journaling Your Progress

You don't actually need anybody else to have accountability. You can be accountable to yourself by keeping a journal. You can do this publicly by keeping a blog, or you can simply write daily in a notebook. Writing it down has several other benefits as well, like letting you see your progress day by day and helping to clarify your goals and what you're doing to reach them.

The More Accountability, the Better

The best strategy is to take a few of these methods and combine them. Write in your journal and also keep a running commentary on your social media sites. Ask a friend to be your accountability partner while also drawing support from an online group. The more support you can get, the better.

Motivate Yourself by Measuring Success

"Never mistake activity for achievement."

– John Wooden

When you first start a new training program or course, you're enthusiastic and excited. It's a whole new world for you. But after weeks of challenges and difficulties, your motivation starts to wane and it's easy to get knocked off track. Having a system for accountability can help you stick to your plan, but it won't necessarily maintain the initial spark of your enthusiasm.

The best way to stay motivated is to chart your progress. When your motivation weakens, you can look back and see how far you've come. You'll be impressed with yourself and it'll seem like too much of a shame to quit now.

What You've Learned

It's important to keep track of what you've learned. A great way to do this is by keeping a journal. Your journal entries can be as short as you'd like, but make sure to note what progress you've made.

When you need motivation, go back into the early pages of your journal. You'll see yourself weeks or months ago struggling with the very basics. It's like a high school kid looking at their books from kindergarten. This will put things in perspective for you and give you renewed inspiration.

What You've Implemented

Looking back at what you've implemented is even more powerful. You should also include this in your journal. When you use what you've learned, you get results. No matter how small these results may be, they'll help you stay motivated. You'll see how what you're learning has an impact in real life. Keep a list of concrete actions and their results.

The Effect on Your Business and Life

Another strategy that helps you see your progress is to ask yourself whether you're better off today than you were before you started. The answer is sure to be 'yes.' For example, if you've been taking a course on starting your online business and it's just starting to get off the ground, this should give you a spark of inspiration. No matter how meager the change for the better is, it's still a change for the better.

Teaching What You've Learned

A great way to measure your success and also reinforce what you've learned is to teach others. When you teach a subject, you have to know it thoroughly front and back. You'll discover where the gaps in your knowledge are, and you can go back and study these. You know you've mastered a skill when you're able to effectively teach others to implement the same thing. One good way to teach others is by blogging about the topic.

Look for Evidence of Success

Whenever you look back over your progress, look for evidence of success. Too often we look for evidence of failure, or we fail to see the obvious instances of success that are staring us in the face. Think positively and look for achievements that demonstrate that you have implemented what you learned. Write them down on your own personal "brag sheet" so you can refer back to them when teaching others also.

The Next Steps

Now that we've been through all the steps you need to take to ensure that any learning you do results in success, it's time to put it all to work for you.

As we discussed at the beginning of this report, there are two main challenges that most entrepreneurs need to overcome:

❏ Becoming addicted to learning all the time

❏ Always learning, but never implementing it

Your job now is to make sure you overcome these challenges and ensure they don't hold you back. Here are the steps you need to take to ensure success:

1. Establish a Mindset for Success

2. Figure Out What You Need to Know

3. Prioritize Your Learning Needs

4. Take Stock and Create a Resource Inventory

5. Choose the Right Training Program

6. Set Objectives Before You Start Learning

7. Limit Your Learning Time

8. Hold Yourself Accountable and Get It Done

9. Motivate Yourself by Measuring Success

10. Get Back on Track When You Wander Off

Action Steps:

❑ Visit www.fireyour.agency/guide to download your Action Guide.

❑ Use the Personal Development Plan worksheet to organize your workflow for learning priorities.

❑ Identify and make a list of the most important tasks you need to do and prioritize the ones that will lead to the biggest potential payoff. Add deadlines for each one.

Chapter 5

. . . .

Step Out of Your Comfort Zone

Forget the Status Quo and Watch Your Business Grow

Growth is something all people strive for, both in their personal and professional lives. In business, growth leads to new ideas and opportunities. To make progress, you need to depart from the status quo and take risks that push your limits – but for most, that's easier said than done.

Your comfort zone is where you feel safe and secure, so leaving it can be terrifying. However, outside of that zone is where true growth occurs. In this report, you will learn how to step outside of your comfort zone and foster the "change mindset" in yourself and your team.

The Change Mindset

How do you step out of your comfort zone and face challenges? You do it by shifting your mindset to turn that terrifying task into a challenge and a learning experience. You do it step-by-step by adding it gradually into your daily routine. You do it by learning strategies to help overcome fear and embrace change. The end result is a whole new potential for growth.

The future is not yet written. You have the power to write it yourself. But you have to step outside your comfort zone in order to get there.

Learning Objectives:

By the time you complete this module, you'll be able to:

- ☐ Smash the status quo so you can move forward.

- ☐ Identify your fears so you can develop a mindset for change.

- ☐ Step out of your comfort zone so you can inspire and facilitate those around you.

- ☐ Make your new change mindset part of your daily routine so it becomes easy for you.

Develop a Mindset for Change

The change mindset accepts and even welcomes fear and challenges. In order to shift your mindset to a mindset for change, you need to identify the fears that are holding you back in any situation and confront them.

Why Do We Fear Change?

As we mentioned at the beginning of the report, our natural instincts use fear to protect us from danger. But there are other reasons we fear change:

- ❑ Change means leaving something you're invested in. You've worked hard to build your systems up to this point, and to change feels like you're abandoning them.

- ❑ Changing means leaving certainty. You do what you do because it has worked in the past. You can rely on it.

- ❑ When we change, we feel like we're losing something. Instead of seeing change as the opportunity to gain something valuable, we see it as the risk to lose something.

These fears are true not only for negative changes, but also positive changes. Even if you're leaving a so-so job for one you think will be great for you, you still feel unsure. You're making a move to a big city where you've always wanted to live, but these doubts are nagging at your mind, even though you're excited.

In this module, you'll learn two strategies to help you confront your fears and make the changes you want to make confidently. It's only this fear that's holding you back from moving forward.

Identify Your Fear

The first step in overcoming your fear is to identify it. When you don't know what it is you're afraid of, you can hardly expect to conquer it.

Here is An Exercise to Help You Identify Your Fear:

Identify two positive and two negative changes that have occurred in your professional or personal life over the past few years.

1. Try to remember how you felt during those changes.

    o   What were the main emotions you experienced?

    o   Were you afraid, stressed, excited, or overwhelmed?

2. Try to remember that exact feeling and feel it again.

3. Then, try to remember what triggered that feeling.

    o   What did that feeling make you do, or not do?

4. Think about what you could have done differently, or what you'd do now if faced with the same challenge.

Envision a Future Free From Fear and Embrace Change

One of the only things we know for certain in life is that change is inevitable. It is one of life's only constants. We can't control change, but what we can control is how we respond to it and deal with it.

Practice Envisioning Your Future

Start by thinking about how your life or business was one year, two years, or five years ago.

- ❑ Write down the most important things in your life at those times.

- ❑ What were your biggest goals and dreams?

- ❑ What were your biggest worries and stressors?

Next, look at the present and the progress you've made since that time.

- ❑ Write down at least three positive changes or things you've accomplished. These could be goals you've met, obstacles you've overcome, changes in the overall quality of your life, or anything else you feel is significant.

Action Steps:

- ❑ Identify 3 things you would like to change in the next year.

- ❑ Visualize yourself at this time next year, having accomplished all of those changes.

Help Your Team Embrace Change

As scared as you are of stepping out of your comfort zone for fear of failure, your team is just as afraid. This includes your employees, your freelance contractors, your virtual assistants, and anyone else you work with on a regular basis. You can lead the charge and facilitate their success by overcoming your fear and showing them how to do it too. In this way, you will inspire your team and become a true advocate for their growth. Here are the best practices for accomplishing this.

Break up Big Goals

If you have big changes you'd like your team to make, take those big goals and break them down into smaller goals so they'll be less overwhelming. Take each item and break it down into small goals that are quickly and easily achievable, things your team can imagine reaching in the short-term. This gives your team quick wins and makes long-term goals seem less daunting.

Anticipate Your Team's Fears

Try to anticipate the specific fears and feelings your team will have about change. In the last module, you already examined your own fears, both in the past and in the present. Do the same with your team. If you can predict the fears they may have when presented with change, you can develop strategies for helping them confront these fears ahead of time.

For example, you might feel that your team will object to a new policy because they feel the old one was working well enough. In order to dispel this fear, you create a simple explanation that shows why you feel the change is necessary, and demonstrate to them that you're implementing the change in a low-risk manner.

Instill the Mindset for Change

In addition to dispelling fears, you can instill in your team the same type of change mindset you developed in yourself. There are several ways you can do this:

❑ **Show your team the benefits of the change they're facing.** This helps them to easily see why the change is positive and necessary. Demonstrate the benefits to both the organization and the team members themselves.

❑ **Show your team they're capable of change by making the transition yourself.** Lead by example and highlight a risk you've taken or change you've successfully made, implying that the same can happen for them. Show them how growth actually works.

❑ **Communicate with clarity and for understanding.** Confusion leads to fear and amplifies it. During a time of change, your team needs to be absolutely clear on the steps to make this change happen and the roles they're expected to play. Make sure they understand exactly what to expect from the process.

Get Resources in Place

Once things start changing, they need to proceed smoothly without any excess stress or confusion for your team. Make sure each team member has all of the resources they need in place before changes start happening. Anticipate the new skills they'll need to learn and teach them these when they need them. You should be there to help by instilling confidence and making the change as smooth as possible.

Reward Successes

If you have a reward system already in place to fit older structures, update it to meet the new needs you'll have. If you don't already have a system in place, create a rewards system to give your team incentives to overcome challenges.

Handling Failures

Let your team know they'll be rewarded for taking risks, but there's nothing wrong with failing. In fact, you should tell them that trying something new and failing is better than sticking to the status quo, because both success and failure are learning experiences.

When you or a team member encounters failure, take the mistake apart and analyze it to try to understand what went wrong. Make it a team activity and focus on solving the problem. Take the heat off the person who made the blunder and look at it objectively. If the failure resulted from taking a chance and stepping outside of the comfort zone, praise this even while analyzing the failure. Turn it into a teaching moment.

Give Your Team More of Your Time

Devote some extra time and energy to your team to help them succeed. Make yourself available for any help they might need. You might consider offering one-on-one coaching sessions or additional meetings when there are big changes in the works. You have experience making changes, and this experience can benefit your team. Through these sessions, you can not only help your team solve problems, but also motivate, encourage, and offer praise.

Take the Focus Off Performance During Times of Change

If you focus too hard on hitting performance quotas, this can hinder risk-taking. You can't leave your comfort zone when you need to issue X number of reports per day. There's no leeway to try something new. Ease off the performance criteria during times when you need your team to grow and change. Performance quotas are the very definition of "status quo."

Action Steps:

Visit www.fireyour.agency/guide to download your Action Guide.

1. Identify one large, potentially scary change you'd like to make in your business (examples could be creating and implementing a new marketing strategy, rebranding your business, or restructuring your team's roles).

2. Break that change down into smaller changes – by creating action steps that build up to the larger goal, it makes the change seem less overwhelming.

3. Anticipate your team's needs – will they need additional training or resources?

4. Be there for your team during the change. It's important that you are available to your team to make the transition go smoothly and help them with any difficulties they run into.

Make Stepping Out of Your Comfort Zone a Habit

In order to see big changes in your business or personal life, you need to incorporate the change mindset into your daily routine. Stepping out of your comfort zone is a habit you develop over time. The more you do it, the easier it becomes. Conversely, if you don't do it often, you'll find it harder to confront your fears. With change as a daily habit, you'll be able to easily face challenges anytime you need to. What's Outside?

What's Outside?

Always keep in mind what's outside your comfort zone. Remind yourself of the benefits and rewards of facing fears and embracing challenges. Remember all of the good things you've learned through your efforts in the past. You may want to write this down and refer to it from time to time, especially when you need motivation.

Do Something That Scares You Every Day

Since leaving your comfort zone becomes easier when you remain in the change mindset, do something every day that scares you. It can be something that just raises your heartbeat a little bit, like starting a conversation with someone in public or making a cold sales call. Don't worry about success or failure - just do it to keep yourself on your toes.

Don't Run Away

Don't run away from fear or discomfort when you encounter it. Maybe you're trying to take more chances in your business life, but you encounter an uncomfortable challenge in your personal life. The two may not be related, but embrace the challenge anyway and see it through. Be aware of your feelings when you feel this way and push yourself to stick with it.

Spend Time with Positive People

Surround yourself with positive people who exhibit the change mindset, and their attitude will rub off on you. You can inspire each other and build a culture of risk-taking and positive change. On the other hand, avoid negative people who prefer sticking with the status quo to facing challenges.

Try New Things

Whenever possible, try new things. Try new restaurants and foods, go to a new workout class, try wearing clothes you don't usually wear. Again, this may not be related to your business or the changes you want to make there, but it will help you stay in the change mindset and influence other areas of your life.

Laugh and Have Fun

Finally, it helps if you don't take yourself too seriously. Learn to laugh and roll with the punches life throws at you. This will make it easier for you to take chances, and you'll be able to withstand failures and mistakes more easily. Having a sense of adventure will make change seem much more fun.

Key Takeaways:

❑ In order to see big changes in your business or personal life, you need to incorporate the change mindset into your daily routine.

❑ Practice embracing change every day and you'll be able to easily face challenges anytime you need to.

Action Steps:

1. Pick one thing you find uncomfortable, but know you'll benefit from.

2. Pick one of the strategies from the module and try it out on that one thing. How did you feel? What did you do differently as a result?

3. Now pick at least 3 other tactics you want to try and 3 things that make you uncomfortable but will lead to the change you want. Mark a slot in your calendar to practice them every day.

Chapter 6

• • • • • • • •

Power Up Processes

Supercharge Your Business and Simplify Your Life by Streamlining Your Systems and Processes

"If you can't describe what you're doing as a process, you don't know what you're doing."

– W. Edwards Deming

To get things done effectively, we use processes frequently in our everyday life. They're a set of linked tasks or activities that produce a result. Even our morning routine may consist of a whole series of processes, starting with something as simple as taking a shower:

- ❑ Turn on shower

- ❑ Wash hair with shampoo

- ❑ Wash face

- ❑ Wash body

- ❑ Wash feet

- ❑ Rinse off well

- ❑ Get out of shower

- ❑ Dry off with towel

And after your shower, you'll have a process for getting dressed. Unless you want to channel your inner Superman, that will involve putting your clothes on in the correct order. Of course, these are very simple examples from daily life, but the principle is the same for business processes.

A business process shows the relevant people in your business exactly how to do something and how to do it as efficiently as possible. It's a well-defined and structured step-by-step process that ends with the achievement of a business objective such as the delivery of a service or product for your clients.

A well-designed business process will simplify and streamline the way that you and your team work together.

Common Areas for Processes in Small Businesses Include:

- ❏ Customer service and support
- ❏ Product development
- ❏ Product launches
- ❏ Recruitment
- ❏ Marketing
- ❏ Managing team members
- ❏ Accounts/cash flow
- ❏ Social media

Business processes in specific areas of your business combine to create a system. So, your marketing system may be made up of multiple processes, each designed to achieve one objective that contributes to achieving your marketing goals.

For example, one aspect of your content marketing might define the process for writing a blog post. The result, depending on your preferred way of doing things, could look something like this:

1. You start with your idea for a topic

2. You research your topic/keyword(s) and take notes

3. Then you create the structure of your post with headings, subheadings, and key points

4. Next, you write the main content of your blog post, filling in the details surrounding your headings and key points

5. Proofread and edit

6. Add images/screenshots and any other visuals to the body of the post

7. Optimize for SEO – including title, categories, tags, internal links, meta description, snippet preview, images, etc.

8. Schedule the post for publishing

Your content marketing system may also include a separate process for reviewing, accepting, and editing guest posts. You may have another system for promoting and sharing blog posts, and yet another for gathering and recording analytics information on your blog posts. You need whatever is relevant to you and necessary for achieving your business goals.

Inefficient business processes are at the heart of many problems facing small business owners. Documenting and optimizing them is the key to remedying those problems.

How efficiently, or otherwise, you run different parts of your business has an enormous impact on things such as:

Your team's levels of frustration, fatigue, and overwhelm

❑ The way others perceive your business

❑ The loyalty of your customers to you

❑ How you spend your time in your business (e.g., putting out fires vs. strategy)

❑ The consistency of your marketing messages

❑ The overall cost of doing business

❑ Your sanity!

When you find ways to simplify, speed up, and streamline processes that you do over and over, you'll have happy team members, delighted customers, lower costs and higher revenue. You'll finally end up with the breathing room needed to focus on moving your business forward.

Your business will have a professional image that helps you gain and maintain a competitive edge. You'll provide world-class customer service experiences, and grow stronger relationships with customers and clients as you spend more quality time with them.

You and your business will be flexible and able to react quickly and efficiently to change or emergencies. You'll reliably and consistently meet deadlines. Profitability, productivity, and quality of work produced will increase exponentially.

Best of all, you'll be able to enjoy the time you spend on your business and have more freedom to spend time outside of your business too. Your business will run smoothly and efficiently without your constant involvement in all its aspects. Your stress levels will plummet as you create a better work-life balance.

Learning Objectives:

By the time you complete this module, you'll be able to:

❏ Identify where you have processes in your business that you perform on a regular basis, so that you can see which ones make sense to focus on

❏ Document or draw out a current, frequent business process that you want to improve, so that you'll know exactly what you're doing now and where it impacts your business and your team

❏ Analyze the process you mapped out, using best practices and input from team members, to identify where the inefficiencies lie and where there's room for improvement

❏ Decide how you will change, outsource, or automate elements of your selected process, so that things run more smoothly and reliably

❏ Map out and document the details of your redesigned process, so that you know exactly how it will work and who will be involved in implementing it

❏ Test your new process to ensure any team members involved can easily and efficiently carry out each step

❏ Communicate and roll out your new process to everyone who is affected by it, so that it becomes part of your regular business operations

Action Steps:

Think about the way you currently run your business and then answer the following questions:

1. Which areas do you feel would benefit most from some focused attention?

2. If you could dramatically improve the way those specific areas run, what impact would that have?

3. Visit www.fireyour.agency/guide to download your Action Guide.

Step 1: Identify Your High-Impact Business Processes

So, you've considered and set down in writing which areas of your business need to be improved, and the impact of dramatic improvements to those areas. Now it's time to take a closer look at the processes within those areas so you can begin to make those improvements.

It seems to be human nature to overthink and over complicate everything. We often create complexity even where simplicity is needed and is more efficient. We say more than we need to because we think it makes things clearer and more valuable. We have a tendency to believe that things should be difficult, so we anticipate things going wrong and want to prepare for that.

This tendency to overcomplicate extends into our business life. The result is that instead of realistic and well-defined business goals (with well-designed processes to achieve them) we have stress, frustration, and inefficiency.

Inefficiency in business commonly occurs in 5 key areas. You may already recognize some of these as areas of your business that are particularly inefficient:

1. HR/Hiring (including contractors or freelancers)

2. Sales

3. Marketing

4. Product Development

5. Customer Service

The key to eliminating inefficiencies in your business is to simplify and streamline by having efficient and straightforward business processes in place. Whether you document and map out the processes to run your business or not, there are probably many processes involved. To make the improvements needed you first need to identify the most inefficient processes.

Identify Processes

Identify where you have processes in your business that have a big impact on your success. Business processes usually come under one of three categories:

Operational or primary processes are the core business processes that deliver value to customers directly. Examples of these include:

❑ Customer support

❑ Product or service development

❑ Marketing efforts including lead generation and nurturing, social media marketing, etc.

❑ Sales

Support processes support your primary processes. They don't provide direct value to your customers/clients but are important because they help you implement your primary processes and achieve your business objectives. These include:

❑ Hiring/recruitment

❑ Training

❑ Technical support

❑ Purchasing

❑ Accounting, invoicing, paying affiliates, paying employees/contractors/freelancers

Like support processes, management processes don't provide direct value to your customers or clients. But they're important to your business because they support your primary support processes and help to ensure your business runs efficiently. They help you achieve your business goals. Management processes include:

❑ Process improvement

❑ Planning

- ❑ Budgeting

- ❑ Getting funding

- ❑ Product planning

The processes that will have the biggest impact on your success are most likely those that fall within the operational/primary category. These are the processes that deliver value directly to customers.

However, success means different things to different people. Success could mean increased income, improved customer satisfaction, achievement of specific business goals, more funding, better training, better working conditions for employees, reduced stress, more time away from your business for you, or any combination of those.

Think about where you have processes in your business. As part of the learning activity in this step, you're going to identify where there are processes in your business that you spend a lot of time on or which have a big impact on your success.

Identify High-Impact Processes for Improvement

Once you have a good sense of what processes you have in your business, you need to identify which are the most inefficient, complicated, or costly. And, even more importantly, which processes will have the highest impact on your business if they can be streamlined.

There are various ways you can do this, starting with asking for feedback and input from team members. You'll get a wealth of information from the people directly involved with the tasks involved.

Also useful is any feedback, complaints, or frequently repeated questions you know you've already received from clients/customers, team members, and contractors or freelancers.

Take time to reflect on the current situation in your business and note problem areas that you already know or can guess are inefficient.

Ask yourself, what is working, and what isn't? For example, are there any visible areas where there seems to be a lack of communication between team members. Are there areas where employees don't appear to have a clear direction or are spending too much time on trivial tasks. Are employee and company targets and deadlines being met?

Where are resources, time, money, etc. being used most? Where are you spending the most time in your business, or on which aspects of a task?

Ask your team members, contractors, and freelancers the same questions.

From those areas that you've identified as having the biggest impact on your success, and those needing the most improvement, choose one business process to focus on for the remainder of the course.

In Step 2 we'll move on to how to document/map out this process. You can then move on to analyze the process and identify specific problem areas to address.

Keep your list of processes that need improving, so that you can return and address them later.

Action Steps:

Visit www.fireyour.agency/guide to download your Action Guide.

1. Complete the worksheet in the workbook. List all the major processes in your business that you feel could benefit from improvement or streamlining. (column 1)

2. For the remaining columns, put a checkmark next to the ones that:

   a. Have the highest impact on the success of your business (e.g., on sales, profits, customer satisfaction, employee retention, product quality, etc.)

   b. Are currently the most inefficient (e.g. in time, money, resource use, etc.)

   c. Have had the most negative feedback (e.g., complaints from customers/employees, questions, etc.)

   d. To help you with filling in the worksheet, get input from team members or others who are affected by each process.

3. Review your completed worksheet and select one high-impact process to focus on for the rest of the course. Note why you picked that process to start on.

You don't necessarily have to select the process that checks off the most boxes. You can also look at which one will be easiest to improve or will have the biggest impact on your business, or even on the stress in your life.

Step 2: Document What You're Doing Now

In this module, you'll work on the high-impact process that you selected for improvement in Step 1. You'll precisely document what you're currently doing in that process, so you have a clear picture of all the steps.

Only when you have a clear idea of how you're currently doing things will you be able to move on to identify exactly where the problems lie, and where you'll be able to make improvements.

Ultimately, the person best placed to document a process is the person who usually carries out the tasks. At the very least it should be someone who has good knowledge about the context of the process, its start and end points, and its objective or outcome.

Now, document your business process as it is now:

Do a High-Level Outline

Start out by going through the process as you normally would, step-by-step, creating a simple bullet point list of the main tasks. This is your high-level outline.

A pen and paper, whiteboard, or Word document is perfectly adequate for documenting at this stage.

Document the Details

When you've finished outlining the main steps, work through your process from the beginning once again, documenting what you do at each step in as much detail as possible.

Write down every action and decision, no matter how small or insignificant it may seem.

Again, you don't need to bother with complicated or fancy tools for this job. Simple pen and paper, a whiteboard or sticky notes. Readily available tools such as a mind map, spreadsheet, Word document, Google Docs, or PowerPoint, will be just fine. Choose the method that is easiest and simplest for you.

Note where activities or tasks in your process are sequential. Look for events that cannot occur until the other is complete.

Note any activities that are parallel. Look for events that can occur at the same time in the process.

Include everything you need to get the job done. For example:

Include links to any resources that will be needed to carry out the tasks. That may include things such as templates, checklists, tools, websites, etc.

Where available or appropriate, include examples of how the finished tasks should look. For example, a completed image for social media created using Canva

Include example text where text needs to input, e.g., tweet content

❑ Any login details that the user of the process will need to carry out the tasks, for example Facebook login information

❑ Include any useful 'front-end' information for tasks, e.g., to give useful background information or reasons why a task is important

❑ If there is essential information that needs to be carried over between steps, make sure to include that too

❑ Identify who does what at each step

Note where screenshots, screencasts or videos of tasks will be helpful for clarity instead of written instructions.

If appropriate, you could even have a colleague or employee take a video while you or a team member completes each task and provides a running commentary of the process. You may have you and a colleague or employee discussing the tasks as they're being carried out.

A very simple initial documented process for a freelance writer hired to write weekly blog posts could look something like this:

 Title of Process: Weekly blog posts for [client name]

Description:

1 x 1000-1500 word blog post per week to be written for [client name and client blog].

[Links to example blog posts]

[Link to any blog post templates or checklists]

Process:

Select Topics

During the third week of each month, the writer and client brainstorm the following month's blog post topics on the client's site Trello board. [login link]

From that list, the client selects four post topics for the writer for the following month.

On a new Trello board for that month, the client lists those posts and the order they should appear.

Write Blog Posts

The writer completes one 1000-1500-word blog post for each week to be ready for client approval no later than Tuesday of each week. Write posts either directly within the Ghost. org publishing editor [login link], or copy and paste your draft post into the platform editor.

The writer formats the post with keyword and topic relevant headings and subheadings. (Dropbox link to document with client keywords)

The writer adds any other formatting including in-post images. Images selected from the client folder on DepositPhotos. (login link and login details)

Client Approval

At least three working days before the scheduled weekly publication day (Friday), the writer notifies the client by email that the post is in drafts on the Ghost platform. (client email address)

The client approves the post or notifies the writer by email of any edits required. Edits can be requested one time only.

The writer makes any requested edits. By Thursday of each week, the writer notifies the client by email that edits are complete and that week's edited post is ready on the Ghost platform. The client is then responsible for scheduling and publishing the post on their blog.

Payment

The writer sends a PayPal invoice to the client after approval of each post. (client email address for invoices)

"

Action Steps:

❑ Visit www.fireyour.agency/guide to download your Action Guide.

❑ Using the examples given in this module as a guide, document the high-impact process you selected in Step 1, so you have a clear picture of all the steps.

Step 3: Identify Where You Can Do Better

In Step 2, you documented all the tasks that currently make up the existing process you've chosen to improve. In this module, Step 3, you'll analyze that process to identify problem areas. You'll decide how you will change, outsource, or automate elements of it so that things run more smoothly and reliably.

When your analysis in this module is complete, you will be able to move on to Step 4 to redesign your business process. That redesign will include all the improvements you identify here in this module.

Define Your Process's Scope

Start by defining the scope or boundaries of the potential changes to your process, so that everyone involved knows what constraints you must work under when identifying areas for improvement.

Documenting now what will not or cannot be done to improve your process avoids future problems such as the addition of resources that are not budgeted for, or the unplanned expansion of the extent of the improvements you want to make. And so avoids the end result of a process that still doesn't match what you need or can do right now.

The types of things you need to consider are:

- ❑ What are your overall budget limitations for improving this process?

- ❑ Are you willing or able to purchase new technology or software?

- ❑ Are you willing to increase your training budget?

- ❑ What's the timescale or time limit for getting this process completed?

- ❑ Can you hire new employees?

- ❑ Are you willing to outsource any aspect of your process? Or change people's jobs or roles?

- ❑ Are you prepared to make immediate changes to other processes? Changes you make to this process may result in it being necessary to make changes to associated processes – consider whether you're prepared to make changes to your other processes now, if not, then specify that in your scope documentation.

Consider all of these questions before you start identifying the improvements you want to make, since they will limit what you decide to do in your redesigned process.

For example, if you don't have the budget to hire a contractor to take over your accounting, then you'll need to look at other ways to improve that process that you can do with your current resources. Or if you aren't willing to increase your training budget, then you'll need to implement changes that don't require much, or any, additional employee training.

As you're working through your process looking for problem areas, it's easier to say no to possible ways to improve if you've already clearly defined the scope of your process improvements.

Common Process Problems

The main problem areas you should look out for are:

- ❑ The process is not clear enough/it's confusing
- ❑ It's too complicated, there are too many steps, and there are irrelevant steps
- ❑ It's too time-consuming
- ❑ It's too heavy on resources

Analyze Your Process

When you are working through the process, ask yourself questions. Or if you're working through this with an employee ask them questions. Make a note of their answers next to each step in the documentation you created in Step 2.

Firstly, ask yourself if there are any steps missing. If so, where, and what? Your work in Step 2 has most likely already uncovered some obvious gaps. Identifying missing steps is a key part of making sure your process will be as efficient and effective as possible so be sure to spend enough time on this part.

Let's look at a very simple example:

1. Write a blog post
2. Schedule it

3. Publish it

4. Promote it

You might think that is a good-enough process. But if someone works through those process steps exactly as you have written them, at the very least they'll find steps missing. Where are the steps for uploading, formatting, proofreading and editing the blog post? All sorts of questions will crop up about what to do next (and how). There just isn't enough detail and information in that process to enable someone to reach the process outcome.

Let's Look At Another Example:

In the hospitality industry, preparing a dining room for hotel guests will include a step for setting the tables. An action called "Set the table," doesn't give enough information to get the job done efficiently. There should also be detailed steps for the correct way to set the table, what items to use, and the order and position to place them.

Getting this process right is not just about making the job easier for your employee, or about making a favorable impression with the customer. Of course, both of these are essential, but it's also about things such as keeping costs down. By using only the number of tableware pieces necessary, this will reduce dishwashing and so save time and money.

If you're wondering how much detail is too much, Marriott Hotels famously has a 66-step manual just for the process of preparing a hotel room for a new guest in 30 minutes!

Remember that your process will ultimately need to be detailed enough for someone to work alone or unsupervised, and to follow it step-by-step to achieve its goal.

Here are some more questions you should ask and answer as you work through your existing process:

- ☐ Are all the steps in the correct or best order to achieve the outcome? For example, could it be completed faster or more easily if you swapped the order of any of the steps?

- ☐ Is a particular step necessary? Can it be removed? What will happen if we remove this step?

- ☐ Where and why does this process slow down or stall?

- ☐ When and why do errors occur?

- ☐ How many employee hours does it take from start to finish?

- ☐ How many employee hours are spent doing work that isn't essential? Could that be reduced?

- ☐ How efficient is it regarding material resources used? e.g., packaging, paper, cleaning products, ingredients, etc. – whatever is relevant to your business.

- ☐ Can I automate the process or parts of the process?

- ☐ Can I outsource the process or parts of the process?

Consider When to Automate

When you have located any problems in your process and removed any non-essential steps, consider which remaining steps could be automated.

The benefits of automation for your business include increased productivity, more efficient use of time and materials, better product or service quality, and reduced workload/work hours for you and employees. However, before you decide whether to automate parts of your process, consider whether automation may complicate your business rather than simplify it. For example, new technology may increase the need for additional employee training to show them how to use it.

Choose software or tools that are easy to use. Some of your team members might not be technically minded, and intuitive and easy to use automation tools minimize the need for time-consuming or expensive training.

Automation is great when it's working efficiently, but have a backup plan in place if the technology fails!

Do not just automate and forget. Monitor your results to check the effectiveness of the automation in achieving its goal, and how well team members are using the tools.

Automation Tools

There are many tools available for automating a wide range of tasks. For example, Zapier is a web automation app that automates your workflow. It can automate tasks that involve Twitter, Hubspot, MailChimp, Wufoo, etc.

Some other tools for automation include:

❑ Finances/accounting: FreshBooks or WaveApps

❑ Email marketing: HubSpot, MailChimp, ActiveCampaign

❑ Social media automation: Hootsuite, Buffer

❑ Analytics: Google Analytics, Kissmetrics

❑ Marketing automation: HubSpot, ActiveCampaign

❏ Task management/collaboration: Basecamp, ClickUp, Asana

Consider When to Outsource

Consider whether you should outsource all or part of your existing process. Outsourcing aspects of your business will free up more of your time for business growth and give you more time to focus on core business activities.

You can maximize productivity and increase efficiency without the expense of a full-time employee, and the readily available technologies for communication and collaboration means you can locate and work with skilled professionals from anywhere.

Examples of Commonly Outsourced Task Types:

❏ Admin

❏ Customer support

❏ Accounting

❏ Social media-related tasks

❏ Blogging

❏ SEO

❏ IT

To identify a process suitable for outsourcing, think about the tasks where your time is least valuable. Conversely, think about the valuable tasks you spend time on. Which tasks are you currently doing that can easily be delegated, freeing you up to work on areas that you either enjoy more or are a more valuable use of your time? What could someone else do just well as you, or even better than you?

Consider the potential drawbacks as well as the benefits of outsourcing for streamlining your business. Primarily, consider if outsourcing will add more work for you. You'll need to make sure contractors or freelancers do what you need them to. You may spend extra time answering questions, explaining things, and overseeing work. Of course, having excellent business processes in place avoids or at least reduces potential problems. Your outsourced employees will know what they need to do to achieve the exact results you want.

Action Steps:

Visit www.fireyour.agency/guide to download your Action Guide.

❑ Decide how you will change elements of your process. To help you decide which elements need changing, use the list of questions provided in the module and work through your process asking and answering relevant questions to identify where problems occur. Complete the worksheet provided.

❑ Work through your process and identify and note any parts (or the whole) where automation will help things run more smoothly and reliably.

❑ Work through your process and identify and note any parts (or the whole) you can outsource.

Step 4: Design Your New, Powered Up Process

You've now picked a current high-impact process to improve and documented it to see how you are doing things now. You've analyzed the process to identify problem areas, and where to make improvements. Now it's time to map out the details of your revamped process so that you & your team know exactly how it will work and who will be involved in implementing it.

Start with the Basics

❑ As this is to be a detailed and complete process document, start by giving your process a title and a description.

❑ Note down the desired outcome of your process. What is its goal or output?

❏ Identify its start and end points. Which activity or task is the first step in the process, and which is the last?

❏ Note the names of team members who will be responsible for completing the activities/tasks.

Document the Details

Map out your redesigned process using the same mapping tasks outlined in Step 2 when you first documented your process (see below for a recap of those tasks). Make sure to include all the improvements you identified during your Step 3 analysis of the process.

Work through the process from the beginning and document each step in as much detail as possible. Write down every action and decision, right down to the smallest. There should be no room for doubt on the part of the person carrying out the actions in the process.

Document any activities or tasks in your process that must be sequential. And document any activities or tasks that can occur at the same time in the process.

Remember that your process design must include every resource and piece of information that you need to make it work efficiently. You will have identified those necessary for your process during your work in Step 2 and Step 3. Refer to that work when mapping out your redesigned process.

Here's a quick recap of some categories you'll have identified you need to include:

❏ Resources such as templates, checklists, tools, and websites

❏ Examples of completed tasks

❑ Login details

❑ Useful background information for tasks

❑ The person responsible for tasks

❑ Details of any visuals such as screenshots, screencasts and videos

The Best Practices for Documenting Efficient Processes

Consider the Length of Your Process

Keep your processes as concise as possible, while still including all the necessary steps and information required to carry out the tasks.

Shorter processes are easier to manage and carry out. So, if it has more than ten steps, consider if it's appropriate to break down into two (or more) processes.

Longer processes can appear intimidating. Employees or team members are more likely to rush through the steps, so it's easy for them to miss important points. Longer processes are also difficult to write clearly.

By necessity, sometimes a lot of steps may be required to achieve the necessary outcome. In these cases, one option would be to consider if it's useful and appropriate for your business to have a short version of the process.

The shorter version could have the general steps outlined (e.g., for people who are already relatively familiar with the process), and a longer more detailed version for anyone new to the process.

Provide Context

Defining your process's position within the wider context of your business, and giving your team members or employees the bigger picture about tasks has various benefits. For example:

❑ It's motivating for the person doing the work as they have a better idea of the value of the work they're doing. It's good to see how the task impacts positively on the business in general, and how it impacts on those who will follow-on and work through the next process in the system or parallel processes.

❑ It also helps you to identify in future if or when the process is no longer needed

Use Visuals

Where appropriate, use visuals to better define the steps. Visuals can expand on written instructions, and demonstrate how something looks when completed successfully. Screenshots with annotations, screencasts, images, and videos, are useful visual elements.

For example, you could demonstrate how to do something such as entering customer data by creating a screencast with a tool like Loom.com

Training videos that show "this is how I/we do it," i.e., exactly how to do something, can be very useful for demonstrating any practical tasks. They can make complicated instructions and tasks easy to understand. Your team members can see every step being carried out and they can see the skills and tools to use. Link to your training videos from your process document.

Make Your Process Teachable

Design your process so that it's simple enough to be understood and taught by anyone. There should be no room for assumptions and guesses, or constant questions and confusion.

More Tips for Writing Your Process

❑ Use simple, informal language and avoid jargon. Make everything very easy to understand. Each step or task should work with very limited or no supervision. It should need little input from anyone not doing the work.

❑ Front-load any useful information that people need to know before they start the tasks.

❑ Provide clear timelines and quality expectations where it's appropriate.

❑ Write your steps so they tell people what they should do, and not what they should not do.

❑ Where possible, anticipate any problems that may occur and include notes or solutions.

❑ Automate where it's possible or appropriate.

❑ Outsource where it's possible or appropriate.

❑ Team members, employees, and freelancers, etc. will change. So, create your processes to be as 'generic' as possible.

Tools for Mapping Processes

There are many tools available for creating flowcharts, mind maps, and other diagram types suitable for mapping your processes, here are some suggestions:

MindMeister

LucidChart

Visio

And of course, there's standard software like Google Docs, PowerPoint, and spreadsheet tools such as Excel. An online search for process map templates will bring up useful templates you can download or use for ideas.

Similarly, an online search for best practices for layout, flow, notation, etc. of your mapped process will bring up useful ideas.

Get Ideas and Input from Internal and External Sources

For help with the redesign of your process, coordinate with relevant team members for their suggestions and feedback. Contractors or freelancers may have experience of similar processes in other small businesses and may have useful ideas to add.

Every small business is different, but some processes are similar or generic across small businesses. For example, developing new products, order fulfillment, customer service support. You can adapt these processes to your own needs and uses. An online search will bring up examples of generic processes you can use for ideas, instead of reinventing the wheel. You may also have colleagues who run small businesses from whom you could get ideas for streamlining generic business processes.

Action Steps:

1. Map out your redesigned process in detail using the Redesigned Process spreadsheet. Include all the improvements you identified during your analysis in Step 3. Include details of any visual elements required, such as screencasts, screenshots, images, and training videos.

2. Create any visuals required.

3. Create any training videos required.

Step 5: Showtime! Test, Implement & Communicate

Now that you have designed your new process with the improvements it needed, it's time to test it out to ensure team members involved can easily and efficiently carry out each step and reach the process goal.

And once you've satisfactorily tested your new process, it's time to communicate and roll it out to everyone who is affected by it. It will become part of your regular business operations.

Test Your Process

When the time comes for your team to test your new process, anticipate, and be ready to resolve, potential resistance to the changes you've made. Make sure your team knows the exact reason for the changes and make them aware of the benefits they will bring.

Pilot Your Process

Before you implement your new process widely, it's a good idea to pilot it first. The pilot gives you the opportunity to gather more feedback, and discover and address any previously unseen problems. Continue to ask questions of the process (see Step 3 if you need a reminder of the types of questions you need to ask), and specifically request feedback from those carrying out the pilot. Note any questions they ask and any steps or instructions where they need clarification.

Based on the feedback you receive during the pilot, edit and improve your new process, and retest.

Involve Your Team

When they're involved and have input into the testing and fine-tuning of your new process, your team members will get a valuable sense of ownership. This involvement makes the implementation easier.

There are various ways you can involve your team in the test phase. Let's look at some of those now.

Perhaps you designed and created the process, but are not the person who will carry it out day-to-day. You need to have the person who will be responsible complete the process on their own, while you watch and take notes. As they work through the steps, make a note of any questions they ask, or problems they identify. Also, note any inefficiencies or problems you identify yourself as you see the process in action.

Have the person who'll be responsible for carrying out the process demonstrate it to another employee, or have them teach another employee how to work through the tasks. These are both good ways of gauging their level of understanding of the new way of doing things.

If it's appropriate, test your new process on someone who doesn't normally carry out the role. The tester could be a new team member or someone on your team who normally has a different role. As before, note any questions they ask and problems that occur.

Depending on the nature of your business, an effective way to check that each step works efficiently and logically is to create artificial but realistic scenarios. For example, if you run a hotel or guest house, have a team member play the role of guest to check the process of booking and paying for a room. In other scenarios, you could have team members play the role of a client or customer and book services, purchase products, make a complaint, and so on. Consider if this a method you could apply in your business.

Measure Your Success

A key part of this testing phase is deciding how you will track and assess the success of your new process.

The metrics that matter to you will, of course, be dependent on your specific process goal/outcome and the problems or inefficiencies it has been designed to address.

For example, you'll want to know if:

- ❑ The new process produces the intended outcome or goal

- ❑ Whether it produces the intended outcome or goal in an appropriate amount of time

- ❑ Your customers or clients are happy with the outcome

- ❑ Whether it's cost-effective

And you might want to measure things such as:

- ❑ Social media metrics, e.g., social followers versus targets, Facebook Page stats, conversions, referrals

- ❑ Sales metrics, e.g., sales growth, profit margins

❑ Marketing metrics, e.g., SEO traffic, SEO keyword ranking, web traffic sources, sales revenue from different marketing campaigns or sources

The metrics you select for tracking your new process will entirely depend on its nature and your goals. So, select from the ideas here or pick something more relevant for you.

Implement Your New Process

You and your team have put a lot of work into creating your new business process, and now it's ready to become a significant and positive part of your regular business operations.

When you're ready to go ahead, you need to let everyone concerned know about the upcoming implementation. You must carry out employee training if needed to make sure everyone understands the changes and can carry them out properly.

To help implementation go as smoothly as possible, be a visible champion of the new way of doing things. Show enthusiastic support for it and commitment to it, and be available to answer any questions that may come up.

New procedures take time to implement and become fully established. Remember to track whether employees seem to be reverting to old methods. If so, remind them of the importance and reasons for the changes. i.e., because of the business problems the old process was causing, and reiterate how the new process will benefit them personally. Ask them why they seem to be resistant to the changes, and whether there are any previously unidentified issues or problems. Provide additional training where necessary.

If you're confident your process is efficient and comprehensive, and your employees are still not reaching its outcome easily, then the problem may be with training or compliance. Provide additional training, and also consider whether you need a better, more effective way of teaching the new way of doing things. Explaining why the changes are important and beneficial is helpful for encouraging compliance.

In the weeks and even months after implementation, continue to track and assess how well the process is working, and whether it's producing the expected results. Be sure to correct problems as soon as they occur.

Once your process is stable and you know it's working, you can again consider automating some tasks to make it even more efficient. Or consider outsourcing. You may also decide to commit to purchasing new equipment or technology to streamline things even further.

Action Steps:

1. Decide how you will test your process. Will you pilot it? What other measures will you carry out to ensure it's effective? Using the worksheet provided, list your test methods.

2. If appropriate, schedule the piloting of your new process.

3. Decide on your metrics for measuring the success of your new process. Complete the worksheet provided.

The Next Steps

Now it's time to review and finalize your redesigned business process and determine your next steps and deadlines. Be ready to implement as soon as you finish the course.

You've Learned:

❏ How to identify the processes in your business which are the most inefficient, complicated, or costly, that you perform on a regular basis. Identifying these enables you to see which ones make sense to focus on for improvement. After choosing one of these current, frequent business processes to improve you then focused on that for the remainder of the course.

❏ Techniques for documenting that process so that you know exactly what you're doing now and where it impacts your business and your team.

❏ How to analyze the process you documented. By using best practices and input from team members, you identified where the inefficiencies lie and where you can make improvements.

❏ How you can change, outsource, or automate elements of your selected process, so that things run more smoothly and reliably.

❏ How to map out and document the details of your redesigned process, so that you know exactly how it will work and who will be involved in implementing it.

❏ How to test your new process to ensure any team members involved can easily and efficiently carry out each step.

❏ Finally, you learned how to communicate and roll out your new process to everyone who is affected by it, so that it becomes part of your regular business operations.

You're now ready to start streamlining your business with your redesigned business process. A business process that will improve profitability and productivity, and help you have a better work-life balance. Once you have implemented your new business process, you need to remember to monitor it closely. Doing so will enable you to identify further areas for improvement.

Action Steps:

1. Make a list of the tasks you still need to complete to finalize your new business process. In particular, you'll need to confirm that relevant team members can easily and efficiently carry out each step to reach the process objective. Set deadlines for each task.

2. Set an implementation target date for your first, revised process.

3. Decide on which process you'll work on next. Use the list of priority processes to be improved that you created in Step 1 to help you decide.

Chapter 7

· · · · · · · ·

Launch Your Product

How To Build Buzz And Maximize Sales For Your New Product Or Service

Why Every Product Needs a Launch Process

For a small business or start-up, a product launch can make or break your profits. The day of your product launch is a crucial one, with a lot of excitement and anticipation, but it also has a big dose of anxiety. If you don't carry out the launch properly, all of the hard work and resources you've put into it will go to waste, and this can mean the end of a small business with limited resources to allocate.

That is why it's vitally important to plan your product launch well. A well-executed product launch plan means more sales and higher customer satisfaction overall.

Taking plenty of time to prepare well for a product launch and deploying careful strategic planning allows a small business on a limited budget to introduce their new products with immediate success.

NOTE: The term "product" used throughout this course can refer to either a product or a service that you are selling. However, some of the tasks will be more relevant to one or the other. When you complete your planning, choose what is most appropriate for your launch.

Learning Objectives:

By the end of this course, you will be able to:

- ❏ Plan and implement the essential pre-launch steps that will prepare you for a stress-free product launch

- ❏ Create the anticipation and buzz that gets your potential customers eager to buy BEFORE your launch goes live

- ❏ Follow a structured process during your live product launch to generate excitement and build maximum sales momentum.

- ❏ Create a plan to continually monitor and accelerate product sales post-launch while ensuring customer satisfaction and loyalty.

- ❏ Use project management best practices that will make your product launch run smoothly, so you can relax and be confident you're prepared to handle anything that comes up.

Action Steps:

1. Write down the next product you will launch. Remember that this could be a service or an actual item you're selling. This product or service will be the focus for the rest of your Action Steps in this course.

2. Set a target date for your launch that is at least two months away so that you'll be able to implement what you learn in this course.

The Product Pre-Launch Phase

We'll be going through the three main phases of a product launch throughout the next three modules:

1. The Pre-Launch Phase

2. The Launch Phase

3. The Post-Launch Phase

If you want to ensure a stress-free launch that also maximizes sales, the Pre-Launch Phase is where you will do most of your hard work.

We're going to cover three key components to the pre-launch that are essential for your success:

1. Laying the Foundation

2. Building Buzz

3. Creating Launch Content

Laying the Foundation

If you already have your product or service completed, you probably also have most of your 'foundation' tasks done. But you may not have prepared them as thoroughly as possible for a smooth launch. So let's do a quick overview of each:

Define Your Target Market

Clearly define the target market that will benefit most from your product. Create a profile of your ideal customer as an individual who you could speak directly to when talking about your product. Your customer profile should include:

❑ Demographic information such as age, gender, location, income, occupation, and so on.

❑ Psychographic information such as fears, worries, hopes for the future, how the person sees themselves, etc.

❑ Behavioral information, especially as it pertains to the products they buy. This includes how often they buy products such as yours, how they feel about the products they buy, what they think is expensive, etc.

A brief example would be: "Joe is a small business owner in the American Midwest who earns $60,000 a year, struggles to balance his time between work and family, and doesn't consider himself tech-savvy. His biggest challenge with his business is finding new ways to connect with his customers after purchasing something. He's tried different ideas in the past, but never has the time to follow through and learn how to implement them."

Develop Messaging for Your Product

From the very start, you need to create clear and consistent messaging for your product or service. This messaging should communicate its unique benefits to the buyer. What need does it address or problem does it solve for your target market? The message you send clearly defines these benefits and communicates them to your target audience.

For example, let's assume that you're selling a project management system for small businesses. You know that your customers find project management systems hard to use, and your main selling point is that yours is user-friendly. Your messaging might be something like: "A simple, no-frills solution for managing your products headache-free." This statement sums up the unique value you offer your customer.

Be careful that your message doesn't make claims your product can't live up to. It's easy to get carried away, listing every possible way your product makes life better for everyone. Put yourself in the shoes of your target buyer. After they purchase your product, how are they going to feel? How will it change their life? Make your message realistic and make sure that your product lives up to its claims now - long before your actual product launch.

Your Marketing Budget

As part of laying the foundation for your launch, you need to create a marketing budget that will cover all expenses leading up to and through the completion of launch. This budget is solely for marketing, not product development. Make sure that all items in the budget are related only to marketing.

It may include things like:

❑ **Public Relations**: Press release development, press kit materials, customer feedback and review program, public appearances, or press tours.

❑ **Digital Marketing:** Online advertising, search engine optimization costs, website development for the product site, or changes to existing websites.

- ❏ **Advertising:** Advertisement in print, television and radio, offline marketing campaigns.

- ❏ **Collateral Costs:** These include brochures, white papers, demos, product samples, training, or other support for your sales force or affiliates.

When setting amounts for your budget, it's always a good idea to pad the costs if there are unforeseen expenses or difficulties.

Create and Implement a Plan for Delivery Channels

Finally, create a plan and schedule for working with distributors, retailers, trainers, and affiliates who will help you promote your product. Create and distribute all of the materials they need to get started and make yourself available if they have questions or concerns.

If you're offering a digital or e-commerce product, make sure that your ordering system and shopping cart work. Test the purchase system yourself early and work out any bugs or problems. You need it to be operating smoothly on the day of your product launch. Make sure all software programs you're using are up-to-date and that none will expire before the launch.

There may be training involved. You might have a product for which your distributors or affiliates need specific training in order to sell. If this is the case, schedule training sessions and prepare the contents of these sessions well in advance of the launch, or even the pre-launch. Add these to your calendar.

Prepare partners, early adopters, influencers, and others who have a stake in the product launch with everything you need them to say and do before, during, and after the launch. This includes giving them any training they need on how to use your product or how to market it, as well as prepared content you'll give them to use.

Building Buzz

The primary purpose of your pre-launch phase is to let as many people as possible know that a new product will be introduced on a specific date shortly and to promote this product heavily to build excitement before it's officially released. This includes the efforts of any affiliates who are also selling the product.

The idea behind your buzz-building strategy should be to get people interested and eager, so that the minute it goes on sale, they're making purchases. The goal is to make each customer want to be the first to buy.

How Long Should the Pre-launch Period Last?

If a pre-launch extends past two months, it's likely to lose momentum and fizzle out before the product launch. This is just too long for the build-up of buzz and anticipation. However, if the product is small, a pre-launch could be only one or two weeks. For our purposes here, we're recommending one to two months. You can think of this as a standard amount of time for a pre-launch.

For creating buzz around your new product so that people will be eager to buy, there are a few things you can do:

Develop a Website Strategy

Create a separate section on your website's main page to create a buzz about the new product launch. This can either be a part of your home page or a link to a new page that offers the latest news about the launch.

The content on this page could be things like:

- [ ] What specific needs it will meet and what benefits it offers

- [ ] The story behind the product. This could be the story of its development, how you got the initial idea, or how it helped a particular customer. A great way to tell this story is through video.

- [ ] Timelines related to the product or its development

- [ ] Feedback from people who have used it in the form of testimonials or reviews

The whole purpose of this page and its content is to interest people in the product. You should update it frequently throughout the course of the pre-launch. During the launch itself, you would then insert a link to a sales page, or redirect the whole page.

Create a Press and Media Plan

You need to craft a press and media plan that alerts people to your upcoming launch and when the product actually launches. Your plan should address three parties: Your existing customers, new prospects, and the general public.

Existing customers are the easiest to sell to and with the least amount of expenditure of resources. What are the best ways to reach your existing customers? If you have an email list, this is a great place to start since email is so personal. You might also communicate with your existing customers through flyers, direct response, or social media (which we'll discuss later). Your efforts here should focus on informing them about the launch and getting them excited about the product.

Your product will also serve as a magnet to attract new customers. They will not only buy the product but also hopefully become new loyal customers as well. Refer to your target customer profile and ask yourself where you're likely to find these people both online and off. Decide where you will find them and how you will reach them.

In addition to targeting the specific types of people you identified in your target customer persona, you should also reach out to the media to inform them about your product.

Traditional ways to reach out to the media include:

❑ Publishing press releases which can be distributed offline to local media outlets and also published online on PR directories

❑ Advertising with local news stations, radio stations, newspapers, trade journals, or magazines

❑ Appearing at local events and trade conferences and spreading the word there

Build a List of Qualified Prospects

Start building an email or contact list of qualified prospects. If you're already selling other products, look at your current customers. If you have an email list, segment the list, and identify which members of the list are qualified buyers.

For example, you might create a segment of your list of previous customers. You could create segments for those who most closely match your customer profile. Another idea is to create a separate segment for people who have contacted you before or who engage the most with you.

A great way to qualify your prospects based on objective data is to offer a free gift that's related to your product. It could be a free download or other digital product that addresses the same needs. Make this offer and see who takes you up on it. Then move or copy them into a list or segment that shows they're interested in this topic.

You can do this with your social media followers, your blog readers, or anywhere else you have contact with your target market.

Try to get feedback from your qualified prospects on how your free gift helped. The people who enjoy the related gift are most likely to buy your product, and you should spend more time marketing to that type of customer.

Create a Dynamic Social Media Plan

Social media is a vital part of your pre-launch strategy. It gives you the chance to update the public in real-time about developing your product and maintain two-way communication with them. You can interact with them through comments, and this helps a great deal in getting them excited and ready to buy your new product.

Some of the types of content you can produce for social media include:

❑ Teaser posts that reveal the product bit by bit

❑ Links to new content about your product such as blog posts or videos

❑ Information on when and how customers can order the product

❑ Posts that share individual benefits of the product

- ❏ Interviews or other content with influencers or celebrities in your niche

- ❏ Purely informational content that's related to your product.

There are many different ways to engage with your audience through social media pre-launch:

- ❏ Create a separate Facebook page linked to your business page. This page will be solely for the product launch and will include updates on the launch.

- ❏ Create a LinkedIn page from your company page where you can post updates and get feedback from your connections.

- ❏ Look for other social media outlets where you can reach new people and generate buzz, such as forums, Twitter, Facebook groups and communities, etc.

- ❏ Provide the product to trustworthy bloggers with big followings, social media influencers, and celebrities in your community, and ask them to mention your product. This is a great way to lend the product credibility, gain valuable feedback, and boost your buzz-generating efforts.

When planning the schedule for your social media, look at signs of engagement such as likes, comments, shares, etc. See what frequency and times get the most interaction and adjust your schedule accordingly.

Build Anticipation with Content

Aside from social media, you can build anticipation and eagerness to buy your new product through any outlet where you can be visible to your prospects. That includes your blog and your email communications.

Create a blog series that's only about this product and documents its development through all of its stages. Promote this blog along with your other content through your usual channels.

Earlier, we talked about segmenting your list to identify potential prospects. During the pre-launch phase, you need to be sending messages to the people on your list to tell them about your product and build excitement. Establish these lines of communication right away.

Create a schedule for all of the emails and blog posts that you will send during your pre-launch, buzz-building period. Experiment with different times of day and days of the week for your communications. Once you start sending out messages, monitor the results carefully.

You'll find your best timing by monitoring and discovering what works best with your audience but here are a few guidelines:

- ❑ Consistency is key. Whether you post or email once a day or three times a week, do it consistently.

- ❑ Weekends, lunch breaks, and evenings when people are most likely to be checking their social media or email are often the best times to post.

- ❑ When marketing through email, look at your open rate, click rate, and other relevant metrics. With blog posts, look at things like bounce rates, comments, shares, and likes.

Again, remember that it's not just about sending out messages and information content during your pre-launch. Try to establish good two-way communication with your audience. This will help to build a relationship with them in which you can get valuable feedback and insights.

Gather Feedback

During the product pre-launch phase, seek as much feedback as possible from your audience and those who have tested or used the product in its beta version.

There are two reasons you need to document your feedback. The first is that you need to use feedback in order to make changes to the product, if still under development, and to your messaging. For example, if those who have used the product think the claims are slightly unrealistic, you need to change your messaging. If your audience responds well to a piece of informational content related to the product or this content brings a rash of inquiries, you'll want to repeat the effort.

The other purpose of feedback is that you can turn it into testimonials, reviews, and other content to spread the word about your upcoming launch. For example, a testimonial from a key influencer or big name in your industry is great to use as part of a press release, or you could fashion an entire press release around it. Testimonials have a big impact as content for your product launch blog or social media pages.

You can gather feedback by:

❑ Conducting surveys with your customers to learn about their problems and preferences.

- ❏ Offering free samples or free trials of the product and then asking customers what they thought.

- ❏ Carrying out a "soft launch" where you conduct a launch of the product or a similar product to one small segment of your market.

Pre-Launch Product Peek

Right before your launch, you should schedule a pre-launch viewing or sampling. You can do this at a meeting place or somewhere online. For this viewing, you can gather key influencers, members of the press, and others with a high profile and a great deal of influence to try out your product and then leak the news to their followers.

This is an excellent strategy for giving your product launch a boost just before it is released to the public. For many members of the audience connected to you, they've heard about this product, and they have some curiosity. A week or so before launch, seeing a key influencer who has experienced the product recommend it, they'll be pushed off the fence and ready to buy when the big day comes.

Ideas for Building Buzz for Your Product Launch

Pre-Launch

1. Submit press releases to PR distribution sites and contact journalists directly

2. Invite influencers to write blog posts about your product

3. Blog. A lot.

4. Be personal with your marketing – focus on the customer, not on your business

5. Create market-focused Facebook ads

6. Create pre-launch explainer videos

7. Promote your tweets

8. Encourage interest through crowdfunding campaigns

9. Incentivize involvement with freebies

10. Use infographics to describe statistical benefits of your product

11. Promote Pinterest pins

12. Offer the opportunity to pre-order at a discount

13. Declare development milestones

14. Create graphics/imagery that are optimized for social media

15. Draw out the suspense for as long as possible

16. Network and promote offline by simply talking to people

17. Offer exclusive early access to loyal customers

18. Give hints... but keep people guessing as to exactly what the product is

19. Use LinkedIn sponsored updates

20. Publish the story behind the product and its creation

21. Advertise any charitable donations you make/intend to make

22. Send out teaser emails to your email list

23. Include social sharing buttons on your lead magnet/ launch page/online material

24. Use contests to encourage interaction even before you go live

25. Offer awards for contest winners, such as discounts/ offers/exclusive access

During Launch

26. Organize a celebratory 'going live' event

27. Ask customers to post stories/videos of their product use

28. Publish how-to videos to explain product uses

29. Publish customer feedback

30. Incorporate customer questions into FAQs and other customer service material

31. Limit sales and incentivize action with scarcity

32. Keep customers informed about sales performance

33. Add bonus materials during launch

34. Add a bonus educational webinar to answer questions

35. Add a bonus one-on-one or group coaching option

36. Offer cross/up/down-selling options of other products/services

37. Continue contests to win the product

38. Create a hashtag for people to use to share their comments

39. Run live, streaming video updates on Facebook

40. Give shout-outs to thank new customers

41. Run an affiliate contest with multiple prizes to encourage more promotion

Post Launch

42. Start building excitement for a future re-launch with a waiting list

43. Create a 'challenge' to get people using your product or service successfully

44. Share success stories publicly and with customers

45. Ask your customers for feedback for future launches or updates

Creating Launch Content

Last but not least, in your pre-launch phase you need to create most of the content that you'll be publishing and sending during the launch itself. By creating this content now, you'll be relieving the bulk of your stress during the launch period. You'll be able to focus on the actual mechanics of the launch and on engaging with customers, rather than scrambling to create things that could have been done in advance.

The idea here is to create as much of your planned launch content as possible. You'll still end up creating more during the launch, as you react to market response and feedback. However, there's a tremendous amount you can do well ahead of time. And of course, there are a few essentials that have to be done for the launch to happen at all.

These include:

Your Product Launch Sales Page

An essential piece of content to have for any product launch is a sales page. This is a page that's solely designed to bring people into your sales funnel. It offers information about the product and launch, and may also include free informational downloads, a chance to sign up for your list or connect on social media, or other ways of qualifying the prospect.

The sales page you create for your product launch may differ from a page that you use going forward, after the launch. For example, if you're planning to offer bonuses that are just for people who buy during the launch, you'll need a unique page that includes those details.

In addition, if you're planning to build anticipation by delivering free gifts and/or videos before the launch, you may create a series of pages that are only visible before the launch. Then they could redirect to the main sales page on launch day.

There are many different ways you can put together your sales page. Your best bet, especially if you're new to this, is to use a template that has already been proven to convert well. For example, InstaPages offers templates ranked by conversion. Tools such as CartFlows and ClickFunnels also make it easy to build your sales pages and sales funnel.

Launch Email Sequence

Aside from the relationship-building emails you send during the buzz-building period, you need to map out and write a clear sequence for promoting your product.

This includes emails just before the product goes live, during the launch period when people can buy the product, and immediately after the launch.

Here's an example of a launch email sequence:

When	Topic of Email
2 weeks before launch	Is [Pain Point] a Challenge for You?
10 days before launch	Want to get a peek at the solution?
7 days before	The Countdown Has Begun!
5 days before	Did You Know that [Product] will [Benefit]?
4 days before	The First Reviews are In!
3 days before	Video - Learn the Secret Behind [Solution]
2 days before	Blog Post - 5 Hidden Benefits of [Product]
1 day before	It's happening TOMORROW!
Launch Day	It's Live! (or) Cart is Open!
Day 1	5 Tips on Using [Product] to Get [Result]
Day 2	Get Your Questions Answered Live (webinar registration)
Day 3	Here's what others are saying…
Day 4	We're Live – All Your Questions Answered (webinar)
Day 5	Tomorrow is the Last Day to [Benefit]
Day 6	Cart Closing… and Final Hours
Day after launch	Join Our Waiting List!
2 Days post-launch	Haven't Had a Chance to Get [Product]? waiting list link
1 Week after	What You Had to Say About [Product]

Your launch email sequence will vary based on how many days you're planning to have the product available for sale, or available with launch specials. However, you can follow this general pattern of anticipation, promotion, and time-sensitive reminders.

Content to Boost Sales During Launch

One great way to build excitement and sales during a launch is to create exclusive content that's only available in that period.

For example, you can add extras or bonuses for early purchases (for example, the first 100). This will entice people to buy early for the extra value.

You can also add bonuses that are just for people who buy during the launch, but you could announce it midway through. You'll provide the bonus for everyone who purchased from the start, but by announcing it a little later, you can give a little incentive to people who have been hesitating.

Also, consider doing something eye-catching to gain attention and create more buzz right when your product releases. This could be a stunt, a new video, or something else that's likely to create a sensation.

Customer Service Content

Lastly, you need to create your customer service content before your launch. This is content that helps customers when they have questions or concerns about your product. It is designed to answer their questions. Examples of customer service content include:

- ❑ **FAQs** – Create an FAQ that answers common questions your customers have had in the past or that you think they might have.

- ❑ **Tutorials** – Make tutorials that teach customers how to use your product.By having customer service content ready during your pre-launch phase, you'll be prepared to quickly respond to your potential buyers and new customers when they have questions. With tutorials, your new customers will get the help they need right away, even while you're busy running your product launch.

Action Steps:

1. Document 5 specific benefits that your product offers your customer. Use these benefits to draft the core messages that you want to communicate in all your launch marketing materials. The message shouldn't be about features, though you will need to include those in the details about your product. Instead, focus on the results a customer experiences after using your product. And focus on the user's experience.

2. If it hasn't already been determined, document how you will deliver your product once it's launched and any technology you need to set up to be able to launch and deliver it.

3. Write down what testimonials you will need to acquire in order to demonstrate your product benefits.

4. List 3 partners, affiliates, celebrities, influencers, or big names who can help you build excitement around your brand. What can you offer these people as an incentive for helping you in your launch promotion?

5. Document what social media and other marketing channels you will use for your pre-launch phase. Eg, specific social media sites, press releases, email, advertising (online and/or print), events, flyers, blog, etc.

6. Make a detailed list of all of the marketing materials and content you need to create for building buzz before

your launch and for during the launch itself. Use the tactics discussed in the module as your guide:

- ❑ What content will you put on your website?

- ❑ What content will you use for press and media buzz?

- ❑ How will you build a list of qualified prospects?

- ❑ What social media content will you post?

- ❑ What other content will you create, such as email series, blog posts, videos, graphics, and slides?

- ❑ How will you gather product feedback before the launch?

- ❑ How will you give people a 'peek' at the product pre-launch?

- ❑ For each piece of content you identified for the launch, outline what you want to include in each, along with a deadline for creating that content. If you'll be having someone else create it, note who that person will be also.

Visit www.fireyour.agency/guide to download your Action Guide.

The Product Launch Phase

The product launch phase is where all of the preparation work you did before comes together to make the actual launch as smooth and successful as possible. Everything should be created and scheduled so that now you're just implementing and monitoring. If all goes well in the pre-launch, you should have a healthy buzz going and your target market should be ready to buy as soon as your product launches.

As we said before, the full product launch can be anywhere from two weeks to three months, depending on the size of the product. Larger products tend to have a longer launch period. The best way to decide on your timing is to look at the norm in your industry. Look at the product launches of similarly sized products in your industry and see how long they usually are.

Keep in mind that products are launching every day. Everyone wants their product launch to be a raging success. But unless you're selling the new iPhone, your first product launch is more likely to involve steady sales over time with a boost on the first day and the last day.

Putting Your Launch Processes in Motion

During the pre-launch phase, you mapped out all of the things that need to be done, and where and when to do them. Now, you're going to implement the actions you identified in the pre-launch phase and expand on them where you see the best reactions.

- ❑ **Marketing activities** – Put all of your marketing plans in motion.

- ❑ **Blog** – While you've been blogging consistently during the pre-launch phase, you may want to ramp up your post count with special content aimed at driving sales around the actual launch.

- ❑ **Tweets** – Like your blog posts, you may want to increase your number of tweets to build up excitement on the eve of the launch. Twitter is all about broadcasting information in real-time, so you can tweet during the actual launch as you watch its progress.

- ❑ **Schedule additional Q&A sessions,** webinars, emails… or other marketing content to address questions or objections that come up during the launch. Problems or concerns need to be dealt with quickly and there are bound to be some once the product is launched.

- ❑ **Increase your social media presence**… mentions, and launch success stories. While you're interacting with people on social media and elsewhere online long before the launch, you should be even more present during the actual launch.

- ❑ **Ensure that distributors, retailers, and affiliates** are using whatever marketing material you've provided and follow up on their sales. Be ready to answer any questions, concerns, or problems they may have during the launch.

- ❑ **Be prepared** to make changes whenever needed either to your marketing or the product itself.

❑ **Make it easy** for customers to learn about your product. As it goes on sale, you should be easily available to inform your customers of the unique benefits it offers. While you may have done free trials to get feedback in the pre-launch phase, the launch itself is also a great time to offer free trials, downloads, and demos.

❑ **Track sales and promote your success.** As you update your audience on social media, tell them how well the product is selling. This serves as additional social proof. Celebrate your milestones with your customers and your internal team.

Customer Responsiveness

During the launch, assuming that you're well-prepared and your systems are running according to plan, you'll mostly be on-hand to offer support not only to your affiliates and partners, but also for customers. This is a vital time to provide customer service.

You should respond quickly to questions and when there are problems, troubleshoot as soon as possible. Although it's more fun to watch your sales climb and promote your launch, you need to make responding to customer issues your number one priority at this stage. How you react to customer issues will have a great influence on customer satisfaction, which translates to repeat sales and positive customer referrals.

When customer issues are publicly aired, your response is even more critical. A customer may post a public comment on social media rather than sending you a private message. When this happens, the issue and your response to it are seen by others who may or may not buy your product. You need to respond appropriately and consider your audience of future potential buyers.

The aim here is to solve customer problems fully and show that you're committed to making sure your customers are satisfied. This will remove barriers of trust that other potential buyers may have. When they see you respond quickly and appropriately to customer issues, they know that they can safely buy from you with no risk.

Make sure there are plenty of ways for customers to reach you. The more communication channels you have open to them, the more effective your customer service will be.

A common mistake that many businesses make with product launches is that they don't have a plan for dealing with a sales surge. What if your launch is an even bigger success than you anticipated, and your sales volume goes so high that you and your distributors can't meet the demand?

If this happens, communicate with your distributors and customers, letting them know that you're doing all you can to meet the demand. Although it's hard for you, this is actually a boon for your marketing. Potential customers will see that your sales are booming, and this helps to show them that you offer true value.

Monitoring and Measuring

Monitoring is also essential during the product launch phase. There are several things you can do to leverage the performance of your launch for even more exposure.

❑ **See who's talking**. Monitor who is talking about your product online and enlist their help. You can sign up for Google Alerts or another notification system so that you're notified each time your product is mentioned. When someone praises your product or tells others about it, enlist them to help you sell more. Ask them for a testimonial or review, offer them a gift, or see if they can help you in other ways.

❑ **Monitor metrics.** Watch your website performance metrics and social media. Analyze which traffic sources are sending the most traffic. Figure out what factors are contributing to your site's performance and maximize these factors.

❑ **Watch customer support tickets.** Keep track of customer support requests and see if there are any consistent issues that you need to address. For example, customers may be having navigation trouble or problems with your shopping cart. Figure out how to fix these issues so that the process will go more smoothly from now on.

❑ **Split-test and monitor.** If you're conducting split-testing on your pages, monitor the results and shift to the high-performing pages when you see a significant difference in conversions.

❑ **Keep track of successes and failures.** Each launch is a valuable learning activity. Keep track of your successes and failures and try to understand the factors that caused them. Keep track of any difficulties or challenges you face along the way. All of this information will be very useful for your next product launch.

❑ **Watch your sales** and offer feedback to your team.

Action Steps:

1. Write down three ways that would make it easy for your customer to experience your product and that will lead to purchase. Add that to the list of things you need to set up or create prior to the launch.

2. Write down a list of potential objections and questions your customers may have during the launch. Add the task of creating answers to those items to your pre-launch content creation list.

3. Document three areas you will measure during the launch that will indicate your level of success.

4. List ways you can increase sales midway through the launch, especially if you are not meeting your sales goals. If you need to create something to prepare for this, add it to your pre-launch activities.

5. Note who will be responsible for key activities during the launch phase, including monitoring social media, customer support delivery of products, answering customer questions and feedback, technology issues, affiliate or partner issues, and delivery of products.

Visit www.fireyour.agency/guide to download your Action Guide.

Post-Launch Priorities

You should see a healthy spike in sales on your product launch day. But if all goes well, these sales will continue and inspire repeat sales and customer loyalty. To achieve this, the post-launch phase is critical.

There are several things you need to do once the product launch phase begins to die down:

Thank Everyone

Take some time to thank all of the people who have helped you make your product launch a success. Thank your channel of affiliates, your partners, bloggers who have written about your product, and influencers who have supported you and helped to get the word out.

While thanking them, provide data that shows how their efforts have helped you. Give them any feedback that might be useful for them. Pay commissions to affiliates either right away or in a timely fashion at the time appointed on your schedule.

Ask for Customer Feedback

Post-sale is an essential time for customer feedback. Once your customers have bought and started to use the product, you need to know how they feel about it. There are a number of ways to gather customer feedback. One is to conduct surveys through email or social media.

You can select individual customers for direct feedback and stories about your product. You can use this feedback to make improvements and also to better understand the relationship of your market to your product. Keep monitoring online for mentions of your name. This is a form of indirect feedback.

Update Instructional Materials

Once the product has launched and you've received actual questions and concerns from your customers, you need to update your instructional materials. Update your tutorials, FAQs, and other teaching materials with these new questions.

Keep Searching for Opportunities

Now that your product is up and selling, you should keep looking for opportunities to promote it to new potential customers. Although you spent a good deal of time doing this pre-launch to identify the best channels and strategies, there are always other opportunities that either didn't present themselves at the time, or that you had simply missed.

Follow-up

Create and implement a system for following up with your customers. This is very important for customer satisfaction, retention, and loyalty. It looks bad for a company if a customer has bought from them and then disappears once the sale is made. Furthermore, you can leverage this first sale for more sales in the future. The customer is now a highly-qualified buyer.

The best way to follow up with customers is through email. Other channels such as social media are good and should be used as well, but email is still the most personal way to connect and research shows it gets the best results.

The point-of-sale is a great opportunity to gain customer emails if you don't already have them. Send the customer emails checking up on them and seeing if they're happy; offering continued support in case they run into problems or have questions; teaching them how to make further use of your product for even better results; informing them of updates; and telling them success stories from other customers.

Ongoing Support

Make sure that at every communication touch-point your customers know that you're there offering support if they need it. Ongoing customer support is a major factor in customer satisfaction and retention.

Keep Watching Metrics

After your initial product launch, sales will most likely decline at least somewhat. The decline could be dramatic, but this is to be expected. However, as you're still looking for opportunities to sell and your product is still out there, watch your metrics carefully and see if there's a correlation between sales and some event or source of traffic.

For example, you might see a sudden unexpected spike in sales a few weeks after your launch. When you check traffic sources, you see that a blogger you hadn't reached out to has blogged a good review of your product. This is a great opportunity to reach out to this blogger and suggest other ways the two of you can help each other.

Gather and Use Social Proof

"Social proof" is customer-created content in the form of reviews and testimonials. It's very valuable because it shows potential customers that you're trustworthy and your product is worth buying. Post-launch, you should be looking for any type of social proof that you can use for your next launch or other content.

A good review by a blogger or another third party is an example of social proof. You can also elicit testimonials from happy customers. There are several ways to do this. The most effective is to contact any customer that praises your product, either privately through a personal email or publicly on social media. Ask them if you can use their testimonial directly for future promotions.

You can also elicit social proof by offering a small incentive, such as a discount or free content. However, you don't want to feel like you're bribing people to say something nice. Only ask truly happy customers to leave social proof. You can also offer those who leave social proof a link back to their site, which helps them get more exposure.

Celebrate with Your Team AND Your Customers

Take some time after your launch to celebrate your success both with your team and with your customers. For your customers, you can hold online events or give away freebies or discounts to say thanks. Focus on making it fun and making sure that your customers understand that you appreciate them.

Start Preparing for Your Next Launch

Once the excitement dies down from your product launch, it's time to start thinking about your next one. Take all of the data and notes you've gathered and get started on your next pre-launch.

Action Steps:

1. Choose the ways you will follow up with customers on their satisfaction, how they're using your product, and to ask for testimonials or success stories.

   Examples include:

   ❑ Direct questions via email, survey, phone call, or face-to-face encounters

   ❑ Contests – Contests you can create include things such as asking customers to send in pictures of them using your product creatively, or to tell a story about how your product helped them

   ❑ Follow up with those who are using your product and retweet or post their messages (with their permission, of course).

2. Outline the key questions you will ask customers post-launch to get feedback.

3. Make a schedule for how often you will check and analyze your metrics, review feedback, and make updates to your product.

The Next Steps

By now, you recognize the benefits of planning and preparing for a product launch in order to get maximum sales, both immediately and in the future.

You've Learned:

- ❑ The necessary steps to a product launch cycle; the pre-launch phase, the product launch itself, and the post-launch activities

- ❑ How to get the word out about your launch and get customers ready to buy in the pre-launch phase so that you'll see maximum sales on the day of the launch

- ❑ What you need to do during the launch itself to ensure that everything goes smoothly

- ❑ The post-launch tasks that need to be carried out in order to maximize customer satisfaction and create further sales

- ❑ The best practices for managing a successful product launch

You also worked though exercises at the end of each module to give you a good start on planning and implementing your first product launch.

Now, you're ready to get started with your first launch. There is a learning curve and you'll take longer to complete all your tasks the first time. There will be frustrations and problems, but here are a few things to keep in mind.

First, choose your affiliates and partners carefully, but also be patient with them. Choosing good partners is a skill unto itself. Some of the people you choose won't pull through or will flake out on you. They may not perform all that you want them to. This could be due to their own shortcomings or a failure in your training and preparation.

Be prepared for mistakes and things that will not go as planned on the launch day. It's rare that everything goes completely as planned, but keep track of problems for future use.

If you're planning a seasonal launch, you should try to do yours ahead of your competitors. Seasonal launches are tricky because everyone is vying for the same day or period of time. This makes seasonal launches especially competitive.

You may want to try a soft launch before your actual launch. This allows you to work out bugs before the big one, gives you valuable feedback, and gives you a good idea of what the product launch will actually be like.

Most of all, keep in mind that your first launch is likely to be slightly rough. In fact, you should expect this. Along the way, you'll document everything well and take note of successes, challenges, and failures. If you do this, your next launch will go much more smoothly and after several launches, you'll be an expert at quickly launching products successfully in your niche.

Action Steps:

Visit www.fireyour.agency/guide to download your Action Guide.

1. Review your notes and what you have learned so far.

2. Determine what you will need to be consistent with tracking and measuring your deliverables in the product launch project plans.

3. Identify the next steps that you will take to finish your product launch planning and start implementation. Assign deadlines and responsibilities for each.

Chapter 8

. . . .

Putting Your Marketing Plan Together

A Step-By-Step Guide for Small Businesses and Entrepreneurs to Get Started with a Marketing Plan

In order for you to know where your business needs to go, you need a roadmap. That's why you create a business plan. The same goes for every aspect of your business, including marketing. In fact, having a clear and thorough marketing plan is essential if you want to maximize your marketing efforts and make the most of your precious resources.

Your business's marketing plan is part of your overall business plan. But while the business plan covers every aspect of your business, your marketing plan deals with only marketing. Your marketing plan includes everything from analyses of your market, your business, and your products, to marketing goals and the strategies that will help you reach those goals.

The key elements of a marketing plan are:

❑ **Market Analysis** – This is a detailed analysis of your market, your customers, your competitors, and other factors.

❑ **Marketing Goals** – A definition of your marketing goals and how they tie in to your overall business goals.

❑ **Marketing Mix** – Your marketing strategy and the tactics you will use to realize your goals in terms of the 4 P's: Product, Price, Place, and Promotion.

❑ **Marketing Budget** – A budget for your marketing expenses and revenues.

In This Module, You Will:

❑ Identify the benefits of creating a marketing plan for your business

❑ Conduct the initial market research that will be included in your marketing plan

❑ Create a company overview that briefly describes what your business is about

❑ Conduct an analysis of your company's current position in the market

❑ Define your key marketing goals and make sure they are in line with your business goals

❑ Decide how you will track whether you are meeting your goals

❑ Gain an understanding of the 4 P's of a marketing mix

❑ Identify your own marketing mix and what resources you need in order to implement it

❑ Draft a prospective marketing budget

❑ Identify your marketing initiatives and calendar for the next year

❑ Determine the key tasks you'll need to do to implement your plan

❑ Identify any next steps needed to complete your marketing plan

By the end of the module, you'll have everything you need to complete your marketing plan and start putting it into action.

The Three Keys To A Successful Marketing Plan

It takes a great deal of investment in time, energy, and financial resources to start a business. This is why starting a business isn't something you want to do in a random, careless fashion. Every effort you make needs to count toward your ultimate goal, with as little wasted effort as possible.

Because you'll be investing so much, it's even more important to create a marketing plan for your business. Your marketing plan is a roadmap for one of the key components of your business – marketing. It helps you refine your strategies and maximize your efforts to get your products in front of the right people who will then want to buy what you have to offer.

In order to complete a successful marketing plan, there are three simple keys. You have to do your research, hone your marketing mix, and monitor your results. This short report will explain each of these keys in detail and give you action steps you can take today to get started.

If you enjoy the report and find it helpful, I also offer a more detailed course that walks you step by step through the process of creating a thorough marketing plan just like the ones that big companies use. But for now, let's get to the three keys.

Key 1 – Do Your Research

In marketing, hard data is everything. You can't base your marketing on your gut feelings or assumptions you have about your market. These assumptions may not be accurate and, in fact, they could be completely wrong.

This is why we conduct market research. Research involves gathering objective data about your market so that you can use it to make informed decisions based on facts.

In years past, before the wonders of the Internet, marketers had to pay large sums of money and invest a great deal of time conducting research. Traditional methods include focus groups, direct mail campaigns, surveys, and one-on-one meetings with customers. These methods weren't cheap. The fact that companies invested so much of their financial resources toward this research shows you just how important it is.

You may feel that you have your finger on the pulse of your market, but the data your research yields may surprise you. Through this research, you need to not only pinpoint the exact demographics of your market, but also how your customers think about your products, your business, other brands they like, and how they spend their money.

There is only one place to get this information. You have to go straight to the source – your market.

Understanding Your Market

An essential part of your marketing plan is to identify your target market. You have to know as much as possible about the people who buy from you. You need to look at large-scale trends among your market as a group, as well as the thoughts and feelings of individuals within this group.

You can gain this data through direct communication with members of your market or through observation. Direct communication, such as conducting surveys or asking questions to members of your market, is very useful. But observation also has its advantages.

When you ask questions directly, a person may feel that they're put on the spot. They may give you the answer they think you want to hear. Observation shows not what they say but what they actually do. It's also very easy to observe your target market online through things like social media, online forums, blog comments, and so on.

What You Need to Research:

- ❑ **Customers.** Get a clear understanding of the demographics of your market, their needs, and what factors influence their buying decisions. You also need to segment your market, dividing it into groups according to important differences within it.

- ❑ **Market Dynamics.** This includes patterns in your market's behavior that occur over time. These patterns could be seasonal, occurring at different times throughout the year, or they could be longer-term patterns that stretch over years or decades.

❑ **Products.** Your research should include what products similar to yours are already on the market. You need to know where your products fit in to the overall scheme of things. It's also important to know what your competitors are offering so that you can offer unique value with yours.

❑ **Industry.** Through research, you should look for current sales in your industry. Each industry has benchmarks which state the best and worst performance level in that specific industry.

❑ **Suppliers and Other Businesses.** Locate suppliers and other businesses you'll need to rely on when your marketing gets underway.

Market research is ongoing. It's not something you do just once and then forget about. You need to constantly research your market because it changes. You'll need to incorporate these changes into your marketing plan.

Next Steps:

❑ Start with some basic research on the above list. Look at the overall economy and current marketing trends. Find out about the people in your market and create a simple profile. Learn about your industry.

❑ Try to look for data that shows trends over time. This is important because you can often get an inkling of future trends by looking at past trends.

❑ Make points of contact with your customers and give them a chance to express their opinions to you. You can do this through forums, social media or other online groups.

Key 2 – Hone Your Marketing Mix

Product — The offering you make to your market

Price — Price range, high vs low, payment plans, pricing options, etc

Place — Where the products are placed for sale

Promotion — Advertising, social media campaigns, live events, etc

Another important element of your marketing plan is what's called the marketing mix. Your marketing mix includes the specific details of your plan. From these details, you can derive the strategies and tactics you'll put into place to reach your goals.

This is referred to as a 'mix' because every business's marketing is different, so you need a combination of factors in your strategy. To define your marketing mix, start with large business goals and work your way down to the smaller details.

Each strategy and tactic is related directly to the attainment of one of your business goals.

An important part of the marketing mix is that it's diverse. You don't employ just one tactic and call that a marketing plan. When you have many diverse tactics, it multiplies your efforts and allows you to reach and effectively communicate with every segment of your market.

The 4 P's

To help you formulate your marketing mix, you should think in terms of the 4 P's:

1. **Product** – Your products or services; in other words, what you're offering.

2. **Price** – The price at which you set the product. This price should conform to the market and its expectations.

3. **Place** – Where you can put your offer in front of your market. This includes distribution channels and all other factors involved in getting the goods to buyers.

4. **Promotion** – How you can promote the product and spread the word.

Product is the simplest consideration. This is what you're offering. Consider the products' features and how they benefit the buyer. Look at similar products on the market and determine how yours is different or better. Try to figure out which unique problem of your market it solves.

Price is fairly straightforward as well, but there's an important point to keep in mind. Your price should be based on the perceived value in the eyes of your market, not the actual cost. This is why it's good to look at the pricing and sales of similar products. Your customers expect to buy a certain type of product at a certain price. You need to price your product according to these expectations. Cheap is not necessarily good if your customers expect the item to have a higher price tag.

Place refers to the location online or offline where you sell your product. The idea is to find out where your target market is and likes to shop and to put your offer where they are.

Finally, there are many different things you can do with promotion. The whole idea is to spread awareness of your product and brand, both online and off. Again, start with your target market. Consider many types of promotions, both online and offline, and determine which kinds would be most effective for gaining the attention of your customers.

Once you have each of these 4 P's defined, test your marketing mix from a customer's perspective. Put yourself in the shoes of your customer and ask questions such as these:

1.   Does it meet the buyer's needs? (Product)

2.   Will your customers consider it priced fairly? (Price)

3.   Will your customers find the product where they shop? (Place)

4.   Will your marketing communications reach them? (Promotion)

Identifying Your Marketing Mix

Here are some questions to help you identify your marketing mix elements.

Product

- ❑ What kind of product does your customer want?

- ❑ What features do your customers want?

- ❑ How will your customer use your product?

- ❑ How big is your product?

- ❑ What color and what shape is your product?

- ❑ What are its functions and features?

- ❑ What is the name of your product?

- ❑ How is your product different from the offerings of your competitors?

- ❑ How will you brand your product?

Price

- ❑ What is the customer's perceived value of your product? (Remember that cost is not an issue in your marketing plan)

- ❑ What are other companies selling similar products for?

- ❑ How do your customers feel about the price you're offering?

- ❑ How do your customers feel about spending their money?

- ❑ How will a small increase or decrease affect sales?

- ❑ What discounts can you offer?

❏ Can you undercut your competition without hurting your bottom line?

❏ Can you offer extra value that would allow you to charge more for the product?

Place

❏ Where do people look for products such as yours?

❏ What kind of store sells products such as yours?

❏ What distribution channels do you need and how can you access them?

❏ Do you need a sales force or intermediaries to help you sell?

❏ Can you sell at trade fairs or other offline events?

❏ Where are your competitors selling their products?

Promotion

❏ Can you reach your customers through traditional advertising channels such as TV, radio, or billboards?

❏ Are there certain times of year when your customers are more likely to buy?

❏ How do your competitors promote their products?

❏ What ideas of your competitors' can you use?

❏ How can you promote your products differently than your competitors?

Product Tactics

Product tactics involve making changes to your products in order to increase their appeal to customers.

Some companies continually put out new products their customers can use. Kellogg's, which is known for its cereal and snacks, makes a wide range of products. It has branded itself as a company that always has new products available for its customers.

Products can be repositioned to meet new customer demands or to attract new customers. They can also be extended to offer more benefits for customers or new segments of the market. New product lines can augment old ones.

One product tactic is to offer special features for your products that other companies don't offer. An extremely simple added feature can make a huge difference to your customers. An example is a fan or heater with a safety feature that shuts it off immediately if it senses someone nearby.

Bundling is another good product strategy. Bundling means putting the product together with other useful products in a 'bundle' to give it added value. An example would be offering free batteries along with an electronic product or a free antivirus software program for a web-design product.

A product tactic that has been gaining popularity in recent years is gamification. Gamification takes some aspect of using the product and turns it into a game for the user. Apps often do this. They offer a reward system or levels that a user passes through.

Language learning app Duolingo takes learning a new language, something that's hard to do, and makes it fun and entertaining with its game-like level system. Zynga's Farmville grew to great popularity in part because of its gifting feature, which allowed players to give each other gifts and grow their farms together collaboratively.

Offering a reward program is a good product tactic. You can reward your product's users when they refer others. One example of a successful referral program is from Dropbox. Dropbox rewards the user for referring a friend as well as rewarding the friend for being referred.

Price Tactics

There is a wide array of price tactics available. Keep in mind that perceived value is an important factor here. Base your price tactics on the expectations of your customers.

You can use competitive pricing or strategic pricing for your goods. Competitive pricing means undercutting your competitors, like the German-owned supermarket chain Aldi, or Walmart in the U.S. These companies operate in industries that are extremely competitive, so they make themselves known for their low prices.

Strategic pricing means charging more than your competitors, but convincing consumers through your marketing that you offer a higher quality product. A great example of strategic pricing is Starbucks, which got Americans hooked on gourmet coffee. Most people would never have imagined paying $5 or more for a cup of coffee, but Starbucks worked the gourmet angle, offering something much higher quality than a typical gas station cup.

There are many more tactics you can use in the domain of pricing, such as tiered pricing that offers customers a variety of options at different prices. This is what Apple does with many of its products, like the iPad, which comes at various prices, each with different features and capabilities.

Market penetration is another tactic in which you offer reduced prices for new products to help them spread in the market. The goal is usually to steal customers away from a competitor who already offers similar products. An example of this is the release of Lay's Stax. Similar to Pringles, Stax were sold at $0.69 at first in order to attract Pringles buyers. Once it had penetrated the market, the product price was raised to its regular price.

The opposite tactic is called **price skimming**. This is where you launch a product at a relatively high price and then gradually lower this price. This tactic is used often in tech markets. Serious tech and gadget enthusiasts will buy the product at the high price because they want to be the first to own it. Once buyers who will pay the high price purchase the item, the price is lowered so that others will buy it as well. This is a tactic used by Sony and other major tech product makers.

Place Tactics

Place tactics are based on how you get your offering to your customers, either physically or online.

For place, you can have locations with high volumes of traffic, online or offline, or try for fewer locations but in areas where consumers in your demographic are concentrated. Your place tactics should revolve around making it easy and convenient for your customers to find and visit you. You should take into consideration the locations of your competitors and other factors such as your distribution network. Accessibility of your location to highways and public transit can be a factor for some offline businesses, as well as ease of access, which includes store layout (again, online or offline) and parking spaces.

Your place tactics may help you expand to new areas. If this is part of your strategy, you'll need to consider each of these new locations and whether or not you'll get the same results there. What works well in one location may not necessarily work well in other locations, even if they seem similar. On the other hand, it may make more sense for your goals if, rather than adding new locations, you instead work to build a stronger distribution network or stronger presence in your single location.

Many retail outlets such as Sony aggressively build locations all over the world where anyone can see and try out their products. Sony's website helps customers find the location nearest them, no matter where they are in the world. While many companies like Sony try to be ubiquitous, others sell their goods only through specialty shops. One example of this is luxury car maker Infiniti, which tailors to a very specific market of high-end buyers.

Under the place category also comes distribution. Will you distribute your products directly to consumers, thus giving you total control over the sale of your goods, or sell indirectly through wholesalers and retailers? The advantage of the latter is that you can extend the reach of your product with minimal cost because you don't have to set up your own sales operations.

Promotion Tactics

Promotion tactics include anything to spread awareness of your company's products. Tactics may aim to increase demand for your product by educating your market on its benefits. Your tactics can boost the image of your brand or communicate the high quality of its products.

Inbound vs. Outbound Tactics

There are two types of promotion tactics – outbound and inbound. As the name suggests, outbound tactics are tactics where you send out your message to get it in front of people. Outbound includes many of the traditional advertising and marketing methods, like television ads, direct mail and special promotional events. These are tactics where you seek out your market.

Inbound marketing is more subtle. It draws the audience's interest rather than sending out a message to them. Many types of online tactics are inbound, such as content marketing, SEO, opt-in newsletters, and sharing content on social media.

Outbound tactics can still be highly successful depending on your market, your industry and how you carry them out. But in general, there has been a shift to inbound marketing for several reasons.

One reason is that it's cheaper and easier to do. Another reason is that people are inundated with so many marketing messages on a daily basis, many outbound marketing messages get ignored. Finally, it simply fits with today's market, where people consume content and base their buying decisions at least in part on this content.

This doesn't necessarily mean that you should forget about outbound tactics and focus only on inbound. Here's a breakdown of the pros and cons of each:

Inbound marketing is successful because it isn't pushy. People don't feel like they're being marketed to. Instead, they feel that they're simply consuming useful information. The downside of inbound marketing is that inbound alone is usually not enough to attract customers. For example, after posting content, you'll often see a spike in traffic but the longer the content is online, the less the traffic will trickle in. It's a passive approach. Marketers often get more dramatic results using outbound tactics.

Outbound marketing takes a great deal more work and resources. But by reaching out directly to your market, you have an opportunity to build stronger relationships with them through this direct communication. It's something of an extrovert's approach. It's more hands-on than inbound marketing. However, it takes a considerable amount of work and is usually costly.

Most marketers choose to use both types of tactics. Using inbound only is like setting up a shop and expecting customers to simply show up. It usually requires some outbound efforts to get the traffic started. On the other hand, even if you focus on only outbound, you'll still need the inbound tactics of good content that customers value so that you'll keep those customers coming back for more.

Offline Promotional Tactics

The most common offline promotional tactic is the advertising campaign. The purpose of an ad campaign is to make you and your product known to the general public. Decide on the specific aim of the ads – whether to sell, inform, brand, or improve your business – and on what media your ads will be seen by your target market. Advertising is usually costly, but it's a great way to get your message directly in front of your market quickly.

There are many ways to promote your products offline through events. You can hold product demonstrations, attend trade shows, give seminars that are both educational and promotional, join and participate in your local Chamber of Commerce, etc. These require a serious time investment but they're great opportunities to communicate face-to-face with your customers.

Another good offline promotional tactic is the free sample campaign. You offer a free sample of your product or service to your target market. This gives them a direct taste of the value you have to offer. If your product is truly helpful and valuable to them, they'll become buyers.

Other traditional offline promotion tactics include direct mail campaigns, selling door to door, telemarketing, and so on.

Since many marketers consider these traditional methods passé in the days of Internet promotions and customers who are more resistant to marketing, many have turned to what are called 'guerrilla marketing' tactics. This includes creative, outside-the-box ideas like leaving sticky notes in public places, writing on the sidewalk in chalk, leaving branded items like pens in public places, and other ways to get people's attention. These are the kinds of things that pique people's curiosity, leading them to ask, 'What is this?'

Online Promotional Tactics

There are many online promotional tactics that take a great deal less effort and cost less than offline tactics. With virtually everyone spending a great deal of time online these days, online promotion tactics that are done well can bring you great results.

Content marketing is a popular promotional tactic. It involves creating content, which can be text-based, visual, video, interactive, or any other kind of content, and using it to build a relationship with your audience. Content can help, inform, or entertain, but it's non-promotional in nature. Rather, it brands your company in the minds of your market, who will then come to you to buy your products and services when they need them.

Email marketing is another good way to promote online. It's often part of a content marketing strategy. It involves obtaining names and email addresses and building a list. You then send informational content along with deals and promotions directly to your subscribers' email inboxes. The advantage of email marketing is that it's the most personal approach, since you are marketing directly to your subscribers' email.

Social media is another type of online promotion in which you create a profile on social media sites such as Facebook, Twitter, YouTube, and LinkedIn, and then make connections with your market there. Again, your activities here should promote in a subtle way. Offer help and information, with a little promotion thrown in. In addition to profiles, you can also create pages, groups, communities, interactive content, and other opportunities for engagement through social media.

Publishing online for Amazon's Kindle or other platforms is also a great promotion tactic. Through publishing informational content that's of interest to your market, you establish your authority in your field. You make a name for yourself and brand your company.

You can also hold online events such as webinars. A webinar is the online version of a seminar where you teach people about something related to your business. Like publishing, this establishes your authority and builds relationships.

Integrating Strategies

It's best to use a wide variety of promotional tactics. Identify the tactics that you think will work best with your target market and choose several of them through several different marketing channels. It's best to diversify because some promotions will fail or lose their efficacy over time, so it's important not to have all of your eggs in one basket.

Action Steps:

Visit www.fireyour.agency/guide to download your Action Guide.

1. Complete the questions on Product Tactics in the Action Guide and draft the tactics you will use to approach the Product portion of your marketing mix.

2. Complete the questions on Price Tactics in the Action Guide and draft the tactics you will use for the pricing part of your marketing mix.

3. Complete the questions on Place Tactics in the Action Guide and Identify where you will 'place' your product/service and distribute it so your customers have easy access.

4. Complete the questions Promotion Tactics in the Action Guide and identify the types of promotion tactics you will use in your marketing mix. Be sure to include

both inbound and outbound methods, such as content marketing and advertising. The Action Guide lists some different methods, so just edit them to suit your needs

5. Draft each of the 4 P's for your business and its products. If you have a segmented market, you may want to do the same for each segment.

6. Test your 4 P's from a customer's point of view.

Key 3 – Monitor Your Results

Just as you need objective data in order to formulate your marketing plan, you also need follow-up data to keep it current. You can obtain this data through monitoring. Monitoring your marketing shows you exactly what's working and what's not so that you can make changes to your strategy. Just as the objective data you discover about your market may surprise you and destroy your assumptions, so can this follow-up data.

Monitoring means not so much watching sales but watching your customers. Like every other part of your marketing plan, it should be based on your customers and their tastes. Once you start your campaign, pay attention to what they say, do and think in regards to your offering and promotions. Watch how they react.

You should also stay abreast of changes in the market or in your industry. These changes could be the cause behind changes in your customers' behavior.

There are many tools available for monitoring the progress of your marketing plan. You just need a few that are good and reliable, and give you the specific data you need.

With these tools in place, you can monitor your marketing by setting goals, milestones, and seeing whether your efforts reach these goals or not. They need to be measurable so that you can tell whether your tactics are working or not. Decide how you'll identify success or failure based on these goals and milestones.

Where you encounter success, replicate your efforts and refine so that they're even more fruitful. For example, if you find that posting a weekly blog increases traffic to your website, keep posting that weekly blog. You may even want to post two per week or add videos to the mix.

On the other hand, where you find results that don't add up, this is where you need to change your tactics. If you're placing banner ads on websites similar to yours and the trickle of traffic they're bringing you isn't worth the money you're paying to place them, this is a tactic you should stop.

Look for weaknesses or gaps. Like your failures, there are areas that can be improved. You can tweak them until they're in line with your marketing objectives.

Next Steps:

- ❏ Track sales, leads, visits to your website, and any other metrics that are related to your marketing goals.

- ❏ Set benchmarks you can reach that will define success for you.

- ❏ Put together a plan for following up with your customers after purchase. Ask them what they liked about the experience and why they left for a competitor.

Why Do You Need a Marketing Plan?

There are many benefits to creating and maintaining a working marketing plan. Once you have one, you'll wonder how you ever got along without it. Here are a few of the reasons a good marketing plan is so essential.

Achieving Your Business Goals

A good marketing plan helps you better achieve your business goals. It puts all of the parts together so that you can implement your plan more easily. It ensures that your efforts will be as rewarding as possible and your money spent in the best way possible. A marketing plan puts together and presents all of the important data you need to make decisions regarding your business's marketing, which is the core of any business's success.

Keeping Up with Changes

If you have a good marketing plan in place, it's easy to alter your marketing strategy and tactics when required. Every market and industry changes, and you may have to tweak your strategy in order to keep up with these changes.

With a solid marketing plan, you can more easily evaluate new opportunities that emerge. A marketing plan allows you to shift your strategy accordingly and stay on track toward your business goals.

A Rallying Point for Your Business

Like your business plan, a marketing plan keeps everyone on the same page. New employees can use the marketing plan to take in your strategy at a glance. The same goes for new business partners and investors. You can easily see where you've been, where you are now and where you're going.

Your marketing plan also offers a rallying point for those involved, including your employees and investors. A good map inspires the crew of your ship and gives them faith in their captain. They can easily understand what you're trying to achieve and how you're trying to achieve it.

Opportunities for Reflection

When you get the marketing ideas inside your head onto paper, you have a chance to see them with a fresh perspective. With everything clearly spelled out, you may notice gaps or weaknesses in your plan that you hadn't noticed before.

Your marketing plan gives you a view of the big picture, and thus more control over your business's marketing. It's absolutely essential for any type of business, whether large or small. So, let's get started writing your marketing plan.

Action Step:

❑ Start your Marketing Plan by listing your long term and short term business goals in your Action Guide.

❑ Visit www.fireyour.agency/guide to download your Action Guide.

If you don't already have business goals, think of them in terms of revenue, costs, operations, and overall business growth. You'll be identifying the marketing strategy you want to use as part of achieving those goals a little later in this course.

Market Research

Market research is an important part of your marketing plan. You need to conduct research because in marketing, you can't afford to make assumptions. You have to rely on hard, objective data about customers. Sometimes the data revealed through research is surprising for businesses that think they understand their customer base well.

Primary Research

There are two types of market research – primary and secondary. Primary research is research where you gather the data yourself. What makes it primary is that you are the one who uncovered it. Primary research may include questionnaires, interviews, surveys, or focus groups where you go straight to your customers for their feedback.

Some ways to gather primary research include:

❑ Asking customers what they think about your products. Would they buy it? How much would they pay for it? You don't have to ask only customers. You can also ask friends, family, or acquaintances for their input.

❑ Visiting businesses that are similar to yours and picking their brains. Depending on your industry and the market environment, some may be quite helpful in giving a new business some direction.

- ❑ Conducting a survey of people in your market either at a relevant offline location or online. 'Relevant' means a place relevant to your business such as a sports club if your business sells sporting goods.

- ❑ Contacting organizations in your industry and speaking to representatives from these organizations.

Secondary Research

Secondary research is where you analyze data that has already been published. There are many ways to conduct secondary research using the wealth of information online.

Secondary research includes:

- ❑ Keyword research – looking at search volume and demographics for certain keywords related to your products

- ❑ Researching competitors, which includes looking at their sites, their products, their marketing efforts online, and their reputation

- ❑ Reading blogs and websites to better understand your market or industry

- ❑ Case studies about your target market researched and published by someone else

- ❑ Joining social media groups and listening to conversations among your target market

- ❑ Looking at reviews on websites like Yelp or Amazon

It's best to conduct both primary and secondary research. Primary research is more labor-intensive for you, but it yields direct feedback that's very useful. Secondary research is easy but not quite as fruitful. However, you can glean important insights through secondary research because the subjects aren't on the spot. They're more likely to be freely discussing their opinions. It's also easier to get 'big picture' data through secondary research.

What to Look for in Your Research

You should look for data related to your customers, competition, and environment. Pay attention to your customers' buying habits and their feelings about what they buy. Focus on the problems they want to solve through their purchases and what deciding factors push them to buy. Find out where and how they like to make purchases.

Study your competition to find out what products and services they offer, and what makes these offerings unique. How and where do they reach out to their customers? Try to learn about their sales figures and in what areas they're having success or not having success. Pay attention to their reputations and how their customers feel about them.

Finally, your research should include the industry and environment in which your company exists. Look for trends in the industry that could affect your sales or reputation. Look for the top selling items and services in your industry and how their sales vary over time. Don't forget to also look at technological changes and how these might affect your market.

Action Steps:

1. What information do you already have about your customers, competition, and environment?

2. Conduct primary and secondary research using at least one of the methods mentioned to complete gaps in your current understanding of your market.

3. Use the Market Research Summary in the Action Guide to keep track of the research that you gather on each of the key areas – customers, competition and environment.

4. Visit www.fireyour.agency/guide to download your Action Guide.

Describe Your Company

Part of your marketing plan is a description of your company. This should include your target market, products and services, unique value proposition, and your mission or vision.

Target Market

Your company's target market consists of the people who will benefit the most from your products or services. This is your ideal customer. It's not someone you hope you'll be able to sell to, but a person who is a good match for what you're offering. If you can clearly identify this person, you know exactly who you need to get your message to, and this maximizes the effectiveness of your marketing efforts.

To define your target market, create a profile for an individual who would be the perfect match for your products or services. This profile should include basic demographic information such as age, gender, location, socioeconomic status, lifestyle, family structure, etc. It should also include psychographic information that includes your target market's worries, fears, problems, values, likes and dislikes, shopping habits, worldview, etc.

Here are some simple questions you can ask to get started identifying your target market:

- ❑ Who are they?

- ❑ Where are they?

- ❑ What do they need?

- ❑ What problems do they face?

- ❑ What do they buy?

- ❑ Where do they buy it?

- ❑ How often do they buy it?

- ❑ How do they make their buying decisions?

- ❑ What is the best way to reach them with your marketing message?

In creating this profile, be as specific as possible. Your company shouldn't and can't be all things to all people. You're looking for the perfect match. If you have more than one ideal customer, make a profile to define each unique segment of your market. For example, your offerings may be of value to people in two very different demographics. If this is the case, split your target market.

Products and Services

What exactly are you offering your target market and what problem does it solve? Identify the specific features and benefits that make it valuable and helpful for your target market. Explain how your products or services are different from similar offerings in the market.

Think of your product or service as a brand. Rather than looking at the nuts and bolts of the product, focus on the benefits it offers your customers and how they perceive it. Describe the image of the product in the minds of your customers.

Unique Value Proposition

Every business should have a unique value proposition (UVP). This is a statement that says clearly, thoroughly, and concisely what value you offer and how it's different from the products of others. Your UVP shouldn't say that you're the best at something, but that you're the only company in the market who does it in this particular way. The UVP explains why your offering is the only one that makes sense for your customers.

Writing a unique value proposition is no easy task. It takes quite a bit of refining until you get it right. Start by brainstorming and answer these questions:

❑ What is unique about your offering?

❑ What specific problem does your offering solve and how?

❑ What are the key benefits of your offering that no one else gives?

Your company doesn't have to be the first one to ever offer a particular product or service. Instead, your product may be unique because it combines two ideas or presents an old idea in a new way. It may be unique because it's the only product of its type aimed at a particular segment of the market. Brainstorm to reveal the uniqueness of what you offer.

Mission and Vision

The statements of your company's mission and vision explain why your business exists and what it does. They explain your business's purpose. This is the framework from which your marketing strategies are formulated.

People often mix up the two terms – mission and vision. However, what you need to know is that a short 'vision statement' is usually one sentence, or even just a few words, that tell the high-level view of where you want to be in the future. Your mission statement can be a tiny bit longer, preferably just a few sentences at most. It gives a little information about how you will get to your vision. You'll have plenty of opportunities to explain in more detail what your business does in other parts of your marketing plan.

Your mission/vision statements should explain who you provide value to, how you provide this value, and, like your UVP, what makes you unique. It's less specific and comprehensive than your UVP and more about the image of your company.

When writing your statements, you can think about the difference between a mission and vision statement as follows:

Mission Statement:

Describes your 'how' for achieving your future, focused on the present. What do you do? What are your purpose and objectives for meeting customer needs?

For example, my mission statement is "To help 1 Million Business Owners become Better Marketers, so they can Build Better & Scale Faster".

Vision Statement:

Describes your 'vision' for the future. Where do you want to be? What does your company's future look and feel like? What are your overall purpose and values as a business?

There are four key elements to a good mission or vision statement:

❑ **It's specific.** Avoid language that is vague or that doesn't tell the customer anything. If it could apply to any company in the world, or even any company in your industry, it's not good enough.

❑ **It's concise.** There should be no fluff. Every word in your vision and mission statements should mean something. Your statement doesn't have to be short necessarily, but every word should count.

❑ **It's clear.** No matter how clever or artistic your idea may be, it needs to be clear and easy to understand for the customer. It's better to be obvious than obscure.

❑ **It's exciting.** This is difficult to pinpoint exactly, but a good mission and vision statement gets the reader excited. Try telling a story, inspiring emotions, and sparking interest with your statement. Ask others to read it in order to get their objective opinion.

Here are a few examples of mission and vision statements from well-known businesses:

Google:

❑ **Mission**: To organize the world's information & make it universally acceptable and useful.

❑ **Vision**: "To provide access to the world's information in one click."

McDonalds:

❑ **Mission**: "To be our customers' favorite place and way to eat and drink"

❑ **Vision**: "To move with velocity to drive profitable growth and become an even better McDonald's serving more customers delicious food each day around the world."

Amazon:

❑ **Mission**: "To offer our customers the lowest possible prices, the best available selection, and the utmost convenience.

❑ **Vision**: "To be Earth's most customer centric company; to build a place where people can come to find and discover anything they might want to buy online."

Nike:

❑ **Mission**: "To bring inspiration and innovation to every athlete in the world."

❑ **Vision**: "To remain the most authentic, connected, and distinctive brand."

Starbucks:

❑ **Mission**: "To inspire and nurture the human spirit one person, one cup, and one neighborhood at a time."

❑ **Vision:** "To establish Starbucks as the premier purveyor of the finest coffee in the world while maintaining our uncompromising principles while we grow."

Action Steps:

Visit <u>www.fireyour.agency/guide</u> to download your Action Guide.

❑ Using the Company Description section in your Action Guide, start filling out the details discussed in this module.

Brainstorm and complete each section carefully, but remember you can return later on if you come across anything you'd like to add.

Assessing Your Business

Your marketing plan should include an assessment of your business. A good way to do this is through SWOT analysis. SWOT creates an analysis of your business in terms of four factors – Strengths, Weaknesses, Opportunities, and Threats.

Conducting a SWOT analysis is a simple step that serves as an important part of your business's foundation. SWOT analyses are simple but comprehensive and this is why they're commonly included in marketing plans.

A SWOT analysis is a 2 x 2 matrix. Strengths are listed in the upper left quadrant. Weaknesses are in the top right. Opportunities are listed in the bottom left and Threats are in the bottom right.

The left-hand column has factors that are helpful in reaching your business goals (Strengths and Opportunities). The right-hand lists factors that are potentially harmful (Weaknesses and Threats). The top two quadrants include internal factors (Strengths and Weaknesses) and the bottom two quadrants include external factors (Opportunities and Threats).

Strengths

Your strengths are your business's strongest qualities. These are both tangible and intangible positive attributes. A good way to brainstorm strengths is to look for areas where you excel over your competitors.

Examples of Strengths include:

- ❑ Keen understanding of niche/Special research resources
- ❑ Highly recognizable brand with strong following
- ❑ Staff who are committed to the company's vision
- ❑ Low production cost for products
- ❑ High traffic location
- ❑ Good distribution network in place
- ❑ Years of experience
- ❑ Reputation for innovation
- ❑ Fast and efficient product development processes

Weaknesses

These are qualities that are under your control but stand in the way of achieving your goals or gaining a competitive advantage. Try to make an honest assessment and don't let pride get in your way. Identifying these areas of weakness is the first step in improving them.

Weaknesses include things such as:

- ❑ Lack of relevant experience
- ❑ Limited resources
- ❑ Lack of access to new technology
- ❑ Current production or distribution methods are costly

- ❑ Small workforce or staff resources already stretched
- ❑ Gaps in capabilities
- ❑ High operating costs
- ❑ Lack of partners or outside help
- ❑ Poor leadership or morale within the company
- ❑ Disorganization or record-keeping problems

Opportunities

These are external factors that keep your business running or could potentially help it grow. This is the exciting part of your SWOT analysis because it shows you areas where you can profit more.

Examples of opportunities include:

- ❑ Market trends that are in your company's favor
- ❑ Changes in society that could make your offer more attractive
- ❑ New emerging technologies
- ❑ Growth in key segments of the market
- ❑ Vulnerabilities of competitors which give you a chance to shine
- ❑ Similar products on the market have clear disadvantages to yours
- ❑ Your products or services may improve local economy, community, or environment
- ❑ Potential partnerships that could prove lucrative

- ❑ Rising or changing customer demand for your product

- ❑ Product or campaign's potential to boost your company's image

- ❑ Seasonal influences

- ❑ New marketing channels you can use to reach your audience

Threats

Threats (or challenges) are external factors just like Opportunities, but they pose a risk or could potentially hurt the future of your business. Although negative, Threats should excite you as well because they indicate a clear direction to go. They show you how you can immediately improve your circumstances and gain an advantage.

Threats can include:

- ❑ Activities of your competitors such as increased sales or exposure

- ❑ Unstable prices in the current market

- ❑ New regulations that affect your products

- ❑ General economic downturn

- ❑ Changes in customer tastes or behavior

- ❑ Bad press for your industry

- ❑ Political instability or world events that could affect your business

- ❑ Environmental problems

- ❑ Similar products that are popular

❑ Time delays due to outside factors

❑ New technologies that could negatively impact your sales

❑ Bad employment market

❑ Competitors moving in on your space or your market

It's difficult to see these Threats as anything but bad, but try to think of them as challenges. If you consider them this way, each Threat can guide you in a new and more lucrative direction.

For both Opportunities and Threats, you're looking for potentialities. These are not necessarily things that are happening now nor things predicted to happen, but they're possible in the future.

Action Step:

Visit www.fireyour.agency/guide to download your Action Guide.

❑ Complete a SWOT analysis of your company and its market using the table in the Action Guide.

Establish Marketing Goals

Your marketing plan should include clear marketing goals. These are not the same as your business goals. Business goals are specific milestones you hope to achieve with your business. They discuss your business as a whole and cover things like overall revenue targets, number of customers, and where that revenue will come from.

Your marketing goals are a subset of your business goals. They outline specific goals you need to achieve on the marketing side of your business in order to reach your overall business goals.

Marketing goals should follow the SMART criteria that we use for business goals. SMART means that your goals follow these standards:

S - Specific

Every goal needs to be clear and simply stated. If goals are vague, there is no way to know whether you've achieved them or not. A good way to make goals specific is to make sure they answer the six 'wh' questions:

❑ What do I want to accomplish?

❑ Why do I want to accomplish it?

❑ Who is involved in its attainment?

❑ Where will this happen?

❑ When will this happen?

❑ Which requirements will be involved in the process?

Of course, you don't need to cram an answer to each of these six questions into the simple statement of your objective, but include all that apply. The objective should be stated in one sentence that anyone with any familiarity with your industry can understand.

M – Measurable

You need a way to measure each goal so that you'll know when it has been reached. Like the Specific criteria, you can refine this by asking 'how' questions such as 'how much,' 'how many,' and 'how will I know when it is accomplished.' Include targets and milestones that you can clearly reach and focus on objective indicators like quantity, time, flexibility, efficiency, etc.

A – Achievable

Goals need to be in line with your capabilities. It may be a challenge to reach your goal and it may stretch your resources, but it needs to be attainable. If it's impossible, you're setting yourself up for failure.

It's not always easy to tell whether or not a goal is achievable at first. Try to consider what work will go into achieving this goal and what resources you'll need. Consider also the time frame in which you want to get it done. It's often easier to see whether a goal is achievable or not once you start working toward it.

R – Relevant

Your marketing goals need to be relevant to your overall business goals. How will attaining this goal help your business move forward toward its goals? Measure each marketing goal against your business goal by asking yourself how it's relevant.

T – Time-Bound

Time-bound simply means that your goals need to be set in a specified time-frame. They can't be open-ended. Your goal may have a time-frame of days, weeks, months, or even years, but it needs to have some kind of time limit. Include a time limit for the goal's attainment as well as specific times for each of the steps needed to reach the eventual goal.

Marketing Goals and Business Strategy

Marketing goals are used to create a strategy. Your strategy will guide how you put your plan into action and it helps you decide which tactics to use. Tactics are the actual concrete methods that will lead you to achieving your marketing goals.

For example, your marketing goal may be to increase revenue from a specific segment of your market by 25%. You'll consider your capabilities, your market, and your marketing plan to decide what strategy will help you do that. For example, you might decide that your best strategy is to increase your presence and engagement on social media to gain access to that market segment.

Once you have a strategy in place, you can draw from it the specific tactics that will put it into action.

Review Your Business Goals

Start with the big picture and work your way down. Review your business goals. Make sure that these goals are clearly stated. Once defined, state your marketing goals, which are tied in with your business goals. Since this is a marketing plan, your marketing goals are the central focus (although your marketing plan should summarize business goals as well).

For now, set marketing goals for one year from now. Where do you want your marketing to get you in a year? Separate these goals into different categories.

When coming up with marketing goals, think in terms of the actions you want your target market to take. When your customers take these actions, it pushes you closer to your business goals.

You can extrapolate your marketing goals into strategy and tactics by asking yourself, 'What can my business do to lead customers to take these actions (the marketing goals)?'

The Purpose of Marketing Goals

Broadly speaking, there are three types of marketing goals. One is to gain new customers. The objective is to get a person to make their first purchase from you. In order to do this, you need people to tell others about you. You need to get the message to them about your offering and its benefits. If you can spread awareness of the unique value you offer, this will result in more first-time purchases. Your tactics should include everything from gaining more exposure to moving customers through your sales funnel toward that first purchase.

Other goals revolve around keeping current customers. Your objective may be to maintain the same purchase amount and frequency. If this objective is met, you'll gain revenue as you gain new customers. To meet this objective, you might encourage increased use of your products or develop new product lines that current customers can use.

Finally, goals can be aimed at getting customers to buy more from you. The tactics would be similar to the last type (keeping customers buying) but the objective would be to increase purchase amount and frequency.

Just remember that your marketing goals should be simple, focused, clear, and should follow the SMART criteria. They should be specific actions you want your customer to take.

Action Step:

Visit www.fireyour.agency/guide to download your Action Guide.

❑ Using the SMART Marketing Goals section in your Action Guide, identify your top 3 marketing goals and check them against the SMART criteria

Track Your Marketing Results

"Measurement is the first step that leads to control and eventually to improvement. If you can't measure something, you can't understand it. If you can't understand it, you can't control it. If you can't control it, you can't improve it."

– H. James Harrington, Performance Improvement guru -

No matter how amazing and ambitious your goals sound, if you can't track them, then you're just shooting in the dark and won't know where to shift your efforts with change.

However, tracking and measuring results is one of the most challenging parts of marketing for many people. It's not as simple as looking at total sales or profit since those can be the result of many different activities, some of which could have nothing to do with your marketing at all.

Your ultimate measure is Return on Investment (ROI). Try to assign specific portions of your marketing budget to specific marketing campaigns in order to make this metric work for you. There's bound to be some impact from one marketing initiative on another, but approximate ROI is better than not measuring it at all.

If you've followed the SMART criteria, you'll already have an idea of what you have to measure for each of your marketing goals. The question now should be the specific metrics to track and how to measure them. Here are a few of the common metrics you'll need to understand in order to measure your marketing results, depending on what goals you've set:

Website Metrics:

- ❑ Unique Visitors – New visitors to your site vs. returning ones.

- ❑ Page Views – The number of pages visitors have looked at.

- ❑ Bounce Rate – How long visitors spend on your site before leaving.

- ❑ Traffic Sources – Where your visitors are coming from (eg, search engines, social sites, email, other pages, etc.)

- ❑ Inbound Links – Other sites that are linking to your content.

- ❑ Keywords – The keywords people used to find your site in search engines.

- ❑ Conversion Rate – How many people perform a desired action after landing on a web page

Customer Metrics:

- ❑ Lifecycle – How long it takes to convert a prospect to a customer in your sales funnel.

- ❑ Conversion Rate – The percent of people who perform a specified action (e.g., sign up for your email list, click on a link, buy a product, etc.)

❑ Average Lifetime Customer Value – How much your average customer is worth in terms of revenue over their lifetime with you.

❑ Customer Satisfaction – The ratings customers give for how satisfied they are with your service.

Email Metrics:

❑ Opens – How many people opened your emails

❑ Clicks – How many people clicked on a link in your emails

❑ Conversions – How many people purchased something after clicking on a link

❑ Unsubscribes – How many people unsubscribed from your list

❑ Subscribers – How many current and new subscribers you have

Social Metrics (vary depending on site):

❑ Likes

❑ Shares

❑ Engagement

❑ Retweets

❑ Repins

❑ Followers

Advertising Metrics:

- ❑ Cost per Click (CPC) – How much it cost you each time someone clicks on your ad

- ❑ Cost per Impression (CPM) – Actually, this is cost per 1,000 times people viewed your ad

- ❑ Cost per Action (CPA) – What the actual cost was to achieve a desired action, such as a sign-up, website visit, like or share.

There are a number of different tools you can use to measure these statistics. There are also companies who specialize in helping you measure your marketing effectiveness. One of the most popular tracking tools, free and available to everyone, is:

Google Analytics

You can track all sorts of information related to your website using the free Analytics tool from Google. When you sign up for an account and tie it to a specific website, you'll receive a piece of code that you'll then insert into your website or anywhere else that allows you to track with Analytics.

Once you've added your tracking code, you'll start receiving data within a few days. You can get data on everything from your Audience to your mobile ecommerce site to social sharing. You can even set goals for your site and track events.

The challenge with Google Analytics is the overwhelming amount of information you receive from Google. To make it easier to track results, try creating your own custom reports by specifying exactly which key metrics you want to track. You can also create your own custom 'Dashboards' for different types of measures.

Check out the pre-designed Dashboards that Google has to see if there are ones that will work for you that are already set up. Just click on 'Customizations' at the top of the left-hand menu, then 'Dashboards', and then 'Create'. Click on 'Import from Gallery' and browse through. A good one to start with is the one from the Analytics Team called 'New Google Analytics User Starter Bundle'.

Keep it simple to start with and gradually explore Google Analytics as you progress in your business. Otherwise, you'll end up wasting hours of time figuring out what to measure and then never get anything done!

Avoiding Overwhelm

The number of metrics you can follow sounds overwhelming, but the key is to focus on just a few and base that choice on your goals. Set just a few measures for your overall marketing goals. Then specify other measures for each marketing campaign or initiative you conduct. You'll be deciding on some of those initiatives later in this course, after you've established your marketing mix. So for now, just focus on the measures for your goals.

Action Step:

- ❑ For each of your marketing goals, determine how you will measure the results, including what tools you'll use and how often you will track the measures.

- ❑ Use the relevant section in your Action Guide to take notes.

- ❑ Visit www.fireyour.agency/guide to download your Action Guide.

Create a Marketing Budget

It's hard to make a budget for the first time, but once you make your first budget and track expenses and revenues, it gets easier. The marketing budget is an important part of your plan.

As a general guideline, your marketing budget should be 1% to 10% of sales. Of course, when you're just starting out, your marketing budget should be whatever you can afford. But if you're a new business, you should expect to spend closer to 10% than 1% on marketing. You may even want to spend more.

Expenses and Resources

To make a budget, make a list of all of your expenses and resources. For expenses, start with fixed costs. These are costs that don't vary depending on other factors. For example, you might have monthly marketing subscription services you pay for or content creators on a retainer.

Then, approximate the costs that fluctuate – your variable expenses. When it comes to marketing, many of your expenses will fall into this second category. If you're running an online ad campaign, for example, you will pay per the number of clicks on your ads (although you can set a ceiling for these).

Also make a list of all of the resources you need to secure in order to carry out your marketing plan. These may be tangible tools you need, such as printing of offline promotional materials or software packages for your online marketing, as well as intangible expenses such as outsourcing.

Allocating Expenses

Decide how much should be allocated to each marketing channel or resource. The advantage of online advertising is that it can be cheap, depending on where you go, and sometimes free. It takes effort on your part to run your online campaign, but there are few upfront charges. Things you might pay for include website design and optimization, pay per click advertising, and advanced tracking software. Offline, you may need to allocate funds for advertising, listings in Yellow Pages or classifieds, direct mail campaigns, and attending trade shows or other events.

Tracking Your Expenses

The most important part of budgeting is tracking. You need to track expenses very carefully. There's a good chance that your first budget will be inaccurate, but if you keep track of expenses well, you can correct for the next budget.

Tracking expenses shows you areas where you need to tighten up and be more efficient. You may find that you're spending a great deal on a particular marketing tactic that is not bringing you much in the way of results. For example, you may be funding a pricey direct mail campaign that's not achieving your marketing objective of gaining new customers.

One thing to pay particularly close attention to is where your customers find you. These are good areas in which to allocate more financial resources.

The marketing budget you come up with will be your minimum budget. It will be increased when you launch new products or expand your business. With your budget clearly laid out in your marketing plan, you'll have the ability to grow when the time comes.

Forecasting Future Revenues and Expenses

The budget section of your marketing plan should include a forecast of future revenues and expenses. This should be based on past financial records along with predictions of market trends and other things that could affect your budget (refer to the Threats section of your SWOT analysis). Once you begin tracking expenses, you can make a more realistic forecast.

For your forecast, it's important to focus on expenses rather than revenues. It's good to overestimate expenses because it reduces the risk that you'll come up short. Double or even triple your projected expenses and you'll protect yourself in case they turn out to be higher. If nothing else, you'll have some left over. Alternately, estimate revenues conservatively. Imagine that high expenses will stay high in the future.

Base your forecast on trends in the industry and have a backup plan in case your sales drop. For example, designate high cost marketing channels that can be put on hold until sales rise again, or find lower cost alternatives to get you through hard times.

Action Steps:

Visit www.fireyour.agency/guide to download your Action Guide.

❏ Using the Marketing Budget spreadsheet provided, estimate your future revenue, based on past revenue and anticipated increases (be conservative)

❏ Next, list current fixed expenses and costs

❏ Next, establish a budget for any expenses associated with each part of your marketing mix. Edit the listed marketing tactics to suit your needs. Make sure your total expenses do not exceed your projected revenue!

Marketing Plan Calendar

All the hard work is now done and it's time to start planning out the actual implementation of your Marketing Plan. Naturally, you'll need to go into more details on action steps once this course is done, but for now you can lay out your high level plans for the year and how and when they'll be implemented.

Your Marketing Initiatives

Start by planning out your major initiatives for the year, based on what tactics you chose in your marketing mix, what your budget can afford, and which tactics are the most likely to help you achieve your goals. For example, an initiative could be to run a promotional webinar series in order to meet a goal of increasing leads by 50%.

Go back to your budget at this point and specify an amount that will be allocated to each initiative. That way, you can keep your costs under control and track your Return on Investment for each initiative as well. Be sure to adjust your budget numbers if you've decided you need more for one initiative vs. another.

Yearly and Monthly Planning

Determine when you will implement each initiative during the course of the year, both on a quarterly and monthly basis, so that you can take advantage of any seasonal trends. In addition, you need to make sure you won't be overtaxing your resources both on the people and financial level. Sure, you can always outsource tasks, but be sure that your own involvement isn't stretched to breaking point.

Goals and Metrics

Set goals for each initiative and determine the metrics you'll use to measure results. Look back at the section in this course on Tracking Results to get ideas of what metrics you can track. An example goal for your webinar series might be to gather at least 200 new leads per webinar. The metrics you track might include webinar registrations, webinar attendance, and any downloads you send your webinar participants to.

Action Plans

Decide on tactics and activities you'll use to implement each initiative. Your 4 P's tactics will help here too. For instance, your webinar series could be free, delivered via Zoom or YouTube Live, promoted via social media, email, press releases, joint venture relationships, etc.

Be sure to identify the resources you'll need for each initiative. For example, a webinar series might require guest speakers, content creators, a new delivery platform, etc.

Finally, complete your action plan by breaking down each initiative even further. Include specific tasks, responsibilities and deadlines. To set deadlines, work backwards from the timing you specified in your yearly/monthly calendars. For example, the creation of each webinar's content will require things like research, slide design, actual content etc. Some of that you may have to do yourself, but many things can be outsourced or delegated.

As mentioned, after this course you'll need to go into even more detail to plan out the specific tasks, responsibilities and deadlines for each tactic and initiative. At this point, you can start by outlining the basics and filling in the rest later – preferably in a project management tool, such as Asana or Trello.

Action Steps:

- ❑ Review your goals and the 4 P's tactics you brainstormed

- ❑ Decide on at least 4 marketing initiatives you want to implement this year to achieve your goals (per quarter). Use the Yearly Marketing Plan Calendar in the separate Marketing Plan Calendar document.

- ❑ Use the Monthly Calendar in the separate Marketing Plan Calendar to outline the timing for those tactics in a monthly format. Some initiatives may span several months, so be sure to note that. Remember to include ongoing marketing activities.

- ❑ Use your favorite project management tool or the separate Initiative Action Plan worksheets to plan more of the details of each initiative, including the goal for each, tasks/activities, resources needed, who will be responsible, and deadlines.

Putting It All Together

You've now come up with a viable marketing mix to help you create a big picture view of your marketing. You've drafted a budget and you've laid out some of the marketing initiatives you want to implement over the course of the year. Now, it's time to put everything together.

Take the action steps you completed and turn each into a section of your separate overall marketing plan document. You can follow the order of modules in this course or change if you feel necessary.

Write an Executive Summary

At the top of your marketing plan should be an executive summary. This is a summary of your entire marketing plan. It spells out the basics and the sections of your plan explain each in detail. The executive summary should be short and concise without any of the minutiae. It should allow the reader to take in the entire plan at a glance.

Although the executive summary goes at the top, it should be the last thing you write. It's much easier to write a summary of what you've already written than what you're planning to write.

Refining Your Marketing Plan

Once you've written a draft of your marketing plan, get as many eyes on it as possible. Ask your team members and colleagues to read it and get their feedback. Ask them if they feel anything is missing or not clearly explained.

Even after the final draft is finished, you should review your marketing plan on a regular basis. Things will change and you'll need to update it.

Action Steps:

1. Use the separate Marketing Plan Template to summarize the work you've done in the course and fill in any missing gaps in your marketing plan. Be sure to add an Executive Summary. If you need to present your summary marketing plan to others, you can use the separate Marketing Plan Overview slideshow as the starting point for putting together your presentation.

2. Review the course thoroughly and use the action plan table in the Action Guide to identify tasks you still need to do to complete your Marketing Plan. Give yourself deadlines for completing these final pieces. You can use the separate Marketing Plan Checklist to see a summary of the complete list of tasks to do from the course and check off each one when it's done.

Visit www.fireyour.agency/guide to download your Action Guide.

Chapter 9

• • • • • • • •

Rapid Results Marketing Blueprint

Finally, Start Getting the Marketing Results You're Looking For

In today's world, there are a plethora of online and offline marketing strategies. Many of them are free or very low-priced, and the majority are easy to implement. When business owners start to learn about marketing, they're likely to download a virtual stack of information products that each teach another strategy "guaranteed to produce results."

Why does all this effort and learning so often produce zero results? The reason is that by leaping in to learn and implement every possible strategy, you get overwhelmed and can't focus on one approach long enough to see results.

Common business wisdom has told us for many years that multitasking is a virtue. The ability to handle a variety of tasks at one time is a valuable quality in an employee or business owner. However, the truth is that multitasking kills productivity, and that includes effective marketing.

Multitasking kills productivity because:

- ❏ It's stressful and difficult to spread your focus in multiple directions

- ❏ Your priorities get confused

❑ Decisions take longer to make

❑ Time is wasted switching between concurrent projects

❑ It's easy for team members to lose focus

❑ The quality of the work suffers

If you try to implement too many projects or marketing strategies at once, you'll increase stress and burn-out, waste resources, diminish progress toward your goals, limit your results, demoralize team members, and in the worst-case scenario, cause your health to decline.

In this course, you'll learn how to use a specific formula called "DISSC" to commit to one approach at a time, and thus gain the benefits of achieving dramatically faster results.

The DISSC Model for Rapid Results is a simple 5-step process to help you focus on one strategy at a time. DISCC stands for:

❑ Define the foundation

❑ Identify your #1 goal

❑ Select your #1 strategy

❑ Specify your action plan

❑ Communicate the strategy to your team

This module is designed to teach you this method and to increase your marketing effectiveness, helping you to more easily reach your goals.

As you work through this course, you will:

❑ Recognize the importance of prioritization and the pitfalls associated with multitasking in your business – including overwork, lack of progress, and poor results

❑ Identify the key steps involved in creating a Rapid Results Marketing Plan that will reduce stress and achieve quick success for one goal at a time

❑ Define the essentials that form the foundation for your success, including your core values, your most profitable products and services, your best customers, and your Unique Value Proposition

❑ Identify your top-priority marketing goal for your business, based on your biggest challenges and your foundation for success – whether it's related to sales, lead generation, or brand awareness - or some other challenge that's been holding you back

❑ Select a single marketing strategy to focus on for rapid results in the next three months, based on how much you're willing to spend, what is easiest to implement right away, what you already know works, what you've wanted to do for a while, or what is the next level to something that has already been successful

❑ Specify the critical elements necessary for successful implementation of the strategy you selected, including top measures you'll track, resources you'll need, top tasks to complete, and regular follow-up dates

❑ Communicate the top goal, priorities, and responsibilities to members of your team through a written plan and guidelines, so that everyone is informed and no one gets overwhelmed or distracted by non-essential tasks

Action Steps:

1. List projects you're currently working on and note the progress you've made on each.

2. Identify where you're getting overwhelmed and why you think that's happening.

3. Identify where you think your team members are wasting time and why you think that's happening.

Define Your Foundation

"It's the job of any business owner to be clear about the company's nonnegotiable core values. They're the riverbanks that help guide us as we refine and improve on performance and excellence."

– Danny Meyer

The first step of the DISSC process is the "D" – Define. Start by defining the essentials that will guide all your marketing decisions. This gives you a clear foundation that keeps you from getting distracted by opportunities that don't align with your true business goals. It keeps you and your organization on track; in other words, you stay true to yourself.

These essentials may change over time as your business grows or adapts to market conditions. When there are major changes calling for it, you should return to this first step of the process and re-define your goals since it's the foundation for everything else.

What Are Your Core Values?

Your core values are principles or beliefs that are at the center of your organization and guide your decision-making. No matter what changes there are in the market - government regulations, the tastes of customers, or anything else in the ever-changing world - these core values remain the same and provide consistency (although as mentioned before, they may be redefined over time, but only with careful consideration).

Core values serve several purposes. They clarify who you are and communicate to people outside your organization what you do and how you do it. They guide you in important business decision-making. They are the essential tenets that keep you true to yourself.

A core value is usually expressed as an adjective that describes some quality of your organization.

Examples include:

- Dependability
- Innovation
- Above and Beyond
- Irreverent
- Results-Oriented
- Anti-Corporate
- Sense of Humor
- Original
- Outrageous
- Commitment to Success
- Traditional
- Customer-Focused
- Hospitality
- Worldwide

How to Define Your Core Values

It's not so much about choosing or creating core values, but rather discovering the values that are already there, leading your decisions. You should be looking for the values that truly lie behind your organization and what it does. Here are a few questions to help you discover yours:

❑ What have been our greatest achievements?

❑ What are common rules my organization follows?

❑ What am I most proud of?

❑ What makes you as a business owner most satisfied?

❑ How do you want people to feel about your organization?

❑ What is most important to you?

The answers to these questions may be full sentences or scenarios. Pare them down to the simplest word or phrase, or the word or phrase that they represent.

For example, "Our greatest achievement is that we've never lost a client." The one quality behind this sentence could be "reliability" or "ongoing value."

Redefining Your Core Values

We mentioned earlier that a time may come when you have to redefine your core values. It might be useful to occasionally review your core values and see if they need an update. There may have been new developments in your business, such as new strengths you've gained, or you may need to adjust to external conditions that have changed.

The process of redefining core values is best done as a group. Gather team members and ask for their feedback. Present them with your original values and ask them if they feel they're still relevant. You can then repeat the process of discovery as a group.

Look at Your Products

Another element of defining the essentials of your business is to look at your most successful products and services.

Start by looking at the range of the products you offer. This could say something about the type of organization you are. For example, the foundation of your business might be that you offer the widest range of choices for your customers. On the other hand, you may be highly specialized.

Look at which products and services are the most profitable. This is likely the area where you want to focus your future efforts. You may decide to put most of your marketing muscle behind these. When considering profitability, don't just look at sales, but also the costs involved for you, including money, time, and resources.

You should also consider hidden costs such as stress and take into consideration your own enjoyment in delivering the product.

Identify Your Best Customers

The foundation of your organization naturally includes your customers – your ideal ones. Identify who your "best" customers are and focus your business on them. Which customers do you consider the most valuable? Remember that value isn't determined solely by profit. Other things that could be considerations in selecting your best customers are:

- ❑ Repeat customers who are loyal to your brand
- ❑ Customers who are easy or fun to work with
- ❑ The level of satisfaction you get from helping them

❏ Customers who are valuable to other members of your organization

❏ Customers who promise future value or benefits to you

❏ Good connections in your industry

Another way to think about it is that these are the customers you want to spend time and effort on. They're the ones that make all your hard work worthwhile and enjoyable.

Why Do Your Customers Buy from You?

Having considered your products and best customers, now ask yourself: "Why do my customers buy from me, and not a competitor?" This is an excellent way to discover your organization's natural strengths.

The specific reason customers choose you instead of a competitor is summarized in your Unique Value Proposition (UVP). Businesses identify a UVP to help them guide all their business and marketing decisions as well. It helps in all areas of business, including sales copy, communications with customers, marketing materials, choice of products and services to offer, and so on.

Unlike your core values, your UVP is one single phrase that sums up these values and the unique benefits you offer your customers.

Your UVP is not a slogan or positioning statement. The purpose is to:

❏ Explain how your products or services solve problems

❏ Tell customers what specific benefits they can expect from using your products or services

❏ Describe what sets you apart from competitors

The UVP should do all of the above while also being as short and concise as possible. It should be clear and easy to understand within seconds.

A template you can use to write your UVP is:

"A (description of product or service) that (what you do) for (target customer) who (their needs)."

For example: "A sales and marketing software platform that's easy to organize for small businesses who don't have time to waste."

You don't have to use this template, but try to write a statement that sums up the above 3 elements. To make your UVP unique, get as specific as possible. Write in a tone that your customers use and can understand. This will also set the tone for your marketing materials and communications with the customer.

Action Steps:

Visit www.fireyour.agency/guide to download your Action Guide.

1. List your core values for your business. Keep this on a separate sheet of paper and post it on your wall as a constant reminder.

2. Fill in the first section of the Rapid Results Marketing Planner:

   ❑ Current products and services

   ❑ Most profitable products and services

   ❑ Best customers

   ❑ Why your best customers buy from you

Identify Your #1 Marketing Goal

"Things which matter most must never be at the mercy of things which matter least."

– Johann Wolfgang von Goethe

It's quite likely that your business has several marketing goals. But for the purposes of focusing and maximizing your marketing efforts, you're going to narrow it down to the one that's most important right now. This goal is the highest priority, and the one that is going to bring the greatest benefit to your business right now.

There's no need to focus on only one goal indefinitely. We're going to concentrate on only one for a three-month stretch. It will be the one clear guiding objective for the bulk of your marketing. Once you achieve this goal, you'll be ready to set your next one.

How to Choose Your Top Goal

The best way to narrow down and find your top goal is to consider the biggest marketing challenge you're facing right now. This is the most pressing problem for you and it needs to be resolved as soon as possible.

There are three main areas you can look at:

Sales

Many marketing challenges are related directly to sales and a company's bottom line. Examples of challenges in this area include:

❑ Your current customers are not aware of other offerings that they may benefit from

❑ You're not seeing as many repeat customers as you'd like

❑ Prospects are not converting to customers at a desirable rate

❑ You're not offering enough variety of products or services that could increase sales

❑ You want to create a new product or service to offer your customers

❑ Prices are too low compared to the value delivered and the cost to create

❑ You want to sell more to existing customers

Lead Generation

Your challenges may revolve around lead generation and nurturing leads, such as:

❑ You don't have a steady flow of leads to reach your sales goal in the timeframe you want to reach it

❑ Your income is unpredictable

❑ You're relying too much on one source for leads

❑ You need a new tactic or marketing strategy to gain leads

- ☐ Leads are leaving your sales funnel at specific points

- ☐ Lead generation activities are costing too much compared to the leads they're bringing in

- ☐ You're not sure how to measure the success of your lead generation efforts

Brand Awareness

Finally, the main challenge you face may be related to simply getting the word out about your brand.

- ☐ There isn't enough traffic to your site

- ☐ Your social media following is small or non-existent

- ☐ Your brand has little name recognition in your market

- ☐ You don't have a strong and clearly defined brand vision

- ☐ It's been difficult to instill your brand vision within your organization among its members

- ☐ Your brand isn't differentiated and unique among its competitors

- ☐ Negative reviews or comments are plaguing the reputation of your brand

Start by brainstorming a list of marketing goals and then narrow it down by putting them in a prioritized list. At the top of this list is the one goal that's most important to your organization right now. This is the goal that will have the biggest impact on your business and your life.

There may be a chronological aspect to your goals. If there's a particular goal that should be focused on ahead of others, make this your number 1 priority for now.

The one you've chosen is the goal you'll focus on for the next three months

Refining Your Marketing Goal

Once you have a simple goal, you need to refine it to make it specific, actionable, and measurable. It's not enough to just say, "Sell more products." You need to decide how much you need to earn in order to know that you've achieved the goal.

A good method for refining goals is SMART goal setting. SMART stands for:

❑ Specific

❑ Measurable

❑ Attainable

❑ Relevant

❑ Time-Based

A good goal is well-defined and focused. Instead of saying, "Get more leads," you should say something like, "Generate a consistent stream of three leads per week that results in at least two sales conversions per month." You can only measure the success of your efforts if your goal is this specifically defined.

Your goal also needs to be realistic and achievable within a three-month period. If it's not, break it up into smaller goals and choose the first of these that needs to be achieved to reach the eventual larger goal.

Action Steps:

1. What's your biggest marketing challenge right now?

2. Visit www.fireyour.agency/guide to download your Action Guide.

3. Fill in the next section of the Rapid Results Marketing Planner:

   ❑ One marketing goal for the next three months

Select Your #1 Marketing Strategy

There are many marketing strategies that are easy to implement at a low cost. As a result, many small businesses and entrepreneurs try to do them all at once, or at least a good handful of them. What ends up happening is that their efforts are spread out and they're bogged down with distractions. Then few, if any, of the strategies end up being very successful.

Now that you have a single clearly-defined goal, you should choose just one marketing strategy that will help you reach that goal. Focusing on just one strategy at a time makes all your marketing efforts easier, more efficient and successful, and less stressful. When it comes to marketing strategies, this is where you'll find yourself most bogged down by multitasking.

Also, remember that this is just for three months. Many small business owners and entrepreneurs find ways to automate, outsource, or delegate strategies once they're up and running. You can simply implement the strategy and delegate it to others, then start your next.

Choosing Your Marketing Strategy

The first step in choosing your marketing strategy is to consider costs. Decide how much you're willing to spend on marketing over the next three months and create a budget.

The best way to make this decision is to first consider your current earnings and decide on a percentage to spend on marketing. Make it a flat amount that you can afford to lose since you can't guarantee that you'll necessarily get a return on the investment, unless you've used the strategy before and you know that it will produce the desired result.

Start by asking yourself questions such as the following:

What's the easiest strategy you can implement right now that doesn't require a great deal of extra resources, training, funding, or people?

❑ What has worked best in the past to achieve the same or a similar goal?

❑ Is there anything that you already know you need to do more of to achieve your goal?

❑ What's on your "most wanted" list of strategies?

❑ If what you're doing now is successful, what is the next step or next level?

When considering marketing strategies, one key factor is the current size of your audience and where you have a following. The right marketing strategy is different for a small business just starting out with no customer base versus a solo entrepreneur with a large social media following.

Here are some ideas for specific strategies depending on the status of your business.

If You're Just Starting Out with Few Customers:

❑ Reach out to affiliates or influential people in your market who have a similar audience and need products or services to promote

❑ Attend networking events and meetups where you can make contacts

❑ Approach blogs whose readership might be interested in your products or services and offer to write guest posts

❑ Create social media profiles and spend some time each day interacting and posting in groups where people can see your profile

❑ Create a high-value piece of content and related lead magnet that you can then drive traffic to and build a list of prospects

If You Already Have a Customer Base:

❑ Try Facebook Ads targeted at current customers or website visitors

❑ Run an email campaign with your current customers to tell them about new or related products

❑ Set up automated follow-up emails telling customers about new or related products after they've made a purchase with you

❑ Offer coupons or special deals that are only for customers

❑ Send out surveys to gather feedback about what other products or services your customers could use, current problems your customers are facing, or feedback on how satisfied they are with your service

❑ Run live product or service creation broadcasts in real-time, based on direct feedback from customers through requests or surveys

❏ Create or streamline the customer onboarding process in order to ensure customers are getting their needs met

If You Already Have An Active Social Media or Blog Following:

❏ Blog three or four times per week and add content upgrades with related offers in your posts, and then promote them across social media using long-tail keywords to identify topics

❏ Conduct a giveaway event through social media or your blog with a related offer

❏ Run a seven-day challenge that relates to one of your products

❏ Set up a newsfeed or alerts so that you're notified of trending topics that relate to your business, and post daily commenting on what's hot right now

❏ Schedule posts for a month ahead of time and check daily, adding time-sensitive news manually. Mix it up between informational content and promotional content so that there's a nice balance of mostly informational content

If You Already Have a Landing Page or Website That is Getting a Great Deal of Traffic:

❏ Run a split test to optimize conversions

❏ Identify your main sources of traffic and look for ways you can increase it. An example would be to increase a landing page's traffic by offering more content or a higher-value product

- ❑ Add visuals and make other improvements to calls-to-action

- ❑ Retarget traffic with related offers. These can be either free or paid

If You Have an Email List (even a small one):

- ❑ If you haven't been sending emails for a while, run a re-engagement campaign

- ❑ Send out a survey to find out your subscribers' main needs and requests

- ❑ Review your email campaign metrics. Look at metrics such as open rates and clicks and try to find ways to optimize subject lines and calls-to-action

- ❑ Segment your list for each product, service, or category to make your content more targeted and relevant

- ❑ Create exclusive offers for different segments of your list depending on their preferences and needs

- ❑ Send coupons to loyal customers as a way of saying thanks

- ❑ Create additional content with helpful tips and high-value promotional offers

- ❑ Create or optimize your customer onboarding to make sure that customers get the results they're expecting

If You Already Have a Tactic That's Working Well:

- ❑ Look for ways to expand or add on to that tactic. For example, if your Facebook group is impacting your sales, consider doing the same thing with a LinkedIn group or running a campaign that will increase the size and engagement of your group.

- ❏ Find ways to better optimize the results of the tactic. If you're getting a great deal of your business through website visitors, employ methods to optimize your top landing pages.

- ❏ Figure out ways to diversify. If you're heavily dependent on referrals for new sales, consider another method such as doing a series of guest blog posts that send people to your lead magnet.

You've been exposed to many different ideas here. Now, with your goal in mind and having considered your current situation, choose one strategy that you will use for the next three months.

As with your goal, you can take a big strategy and break it down into something smaller and more manageable. Also like your goal, devise some way to measure the results of your efforts. You'll need to look at your progress in three months and be able to determine whether the strategy is paying off or not.

Brainstorm a few options and narrow them down until you've found the best one. Before you start implementing it, review your foundations and the answers you gave to the questions in this module to make sure it's the right one.

Action Steps:

Visit www.fireyour.agency/guide to download your Action Guide.

1. Determine how much you are willing to spend on marketing in the next three months.

2. Answer the questions listed in the module.

3. Note which of the other factors listed in the module apply to your business.

4. Fill in the next section of the Rapid Results Marketing Planner, making sure it's in line with the first two sections – your foundation and your #1 marketing goal.

5. Pick one marketing strategy or one step in a larger strategy for the next three months.

Specify Your Action Plan

On the "Rapid Results Planner" you've written down the one marketing strategy you will focus on for the next three months. Now, let's move down the sheet and tackle the next few problems, which involve specifying your action plan.

Track Your Progress

In the last modules, we talked about setting specific goals and strategies so that you can track progress.

There are a number of metrics available to do this. In fact, there are too many. The Internet is great at providing metrics on every single element of a marketing strategy, but this can be overwhelming and waste a great deal of time. Instead, you need to narrow it down to just a small handful of metrics that will tell you exactly whether your strategy is working or not.

Which ones you'll track depends on the marketing strategy you're using.

❑ Examples of metrics to track include:

❑ Conversion of traffic to leads

❑ Conversion of leads to customers

❑ Revenue from new sales to current customers

- ☐ Cost per conversion if using an ad network like Facebook Ads

- ☐ Percentage increase in repeat buyers

- ☐ Email open rates and clicks on links in emails

- ☐ Traffic from social media sites to landing pages

- ☐ Downloads of lead magnet and new subscribers for email list

Engagement with email subscribers or social media followers measured in comments, likes, shares, clicks, and so on

Brainstorm a list of metrics related to the marketing goal and strategy you picked and then narrow it down. Prioritize the list so that you have the most relevant and important metrics at the top. Now, choose only the top three to use for measuring your marketing strategy.

Create a plan to analyze your metrics on a regular basis. Track metrics at a minimum of once a week. Look at your schedule and choose a frequency that works for you.

Specify the Resources You Need

Before you get started, it's important to identify what resources you'll need to implement your strategy and measure results. The key resource areas are:

People

What staff do you need to carry out your plan? Are there any outsourcers, freelancers, or virtual help needed? Will you need tech help? Are there business partners or colleagues you'll need assistance from?

Money

What expenses will you face along the way? Consider things such as ad money, subscriptions, memberships, tools you need to buy, such as software, rental fees, and anything else you'll need to pay for.

Tools

Will you need any software programs, dashboards, physical tools, computers, devices, and so on to carry out your plan?

Training

Are there new skills you or your team members will need to learn?

Coaching

Will you need someone to advise you and walk you through the process?

Brainstorm everything you might need along the way. When estimating costs or the amount of a certain resource you need, padding the amount a little will help ensure against running short. It's better to overestimate what you need than to underestimate and come up short-handed.

After you've considered all the above, what are you currently lacking? If what you need is way beyond your regular budget, you might decide to ditch the marketing strategy you've chosen and go with something a bit more reasonable. If you choose to stick to the strategy you've chosen, there may be ways you can expand your budget to accommodate.

Decide how you will procure the resources you need.

Outline Your Top Five Tasks

Now, refer to your Planner. It's time to create your high-level action plan. These are the key phases of your project and the specifics that will get it done.

For example, if you are creating a new Facebook marketing funnel to attract new leads, your main tasks might be:

❑ Identifying and creating a lead magnet

❑ Setting up your funnel pages and lists, such as your opt-in page, thank-you message, download page, and so on

❑ Writing follow-up emails

❑ Setting up a Facebook Ad to drive traffic to your lead magnet

❑ Monitoring your ad for cost per conversion

Sometimes it helps to create your action steps backwards. It may be easier to envision the goal and then ask yourself, "What needs to happen in order to reach my goal?" Keep asking as you work your way backward and identify each step along the way.

For example, say your goal is to grow your email subscribers to 500 members. How do you know when you've done this? You need 500 people to sign up. On the technical side, you need your landing page, opt-in, and list set up. Then, you need to ask yourself, "How do I get 500 people to the landing page?" This leads to your traffic strategy and all the steps that go into that.

Once you've finished the "Rapid Results Marketing Planner" you'll need to create a more detailed action plan for each of the five tasks. What you'll need to decide is:

- ❏ A breakdown of the detailed tasks involved in each of the major ones

- ❏ A deadline for each task, which you will put on your calendar

- ❏ Who is responsible for completing each task

- ❏ Any additional resources you'll need

If you have team members or others who are involved in implementing your strategy, you should include them in the detailed project planning after you've shared your goal and strategy. This requires more work and consideration, but with everything planned and in place, you'll see how much more smoothly it goes than trying to do everything at once.

Action Steps:

- ❏ Fill in the last sections of the Rapid Results Marketing Planner:

  - ○ Top 3 metrics to track

  - ○ Resources needed

  - ○ Top 5 tasks to complete

  - ○ Dates for reviewing progress

Communicate Team-Wide

Now that everything is in place, you'll need to ensure that everyone on your team is on the same page. They need to be setting the right priorities based on the work you've done so far in this course. They need to be on target with the number one goal, number one strategy, and action plan.

Create Guidelines

Aside from holding meetings and imparting this information verbally to your team members, you should also create documents that explain everything clearly and to which they can refer whenever necessary.

Your guidelines should include:

- [ ] The main goal you're going to be working toward over the next three months

- [ ] The marketing strategy in detail that you will employ to get there

- [ ] All the action steps involved in employing this marketing strategy

- [ ] All resources needed and how you will procure them

- [ ] How progress will be marked through the course of the three months

- [ ] The key responsibilities of each team member

You can either give your team members printed documents or create digital files that they can access at any time. The advantage of using digital files is that you can make changes and updates, which may be necessary as you proceed. Online, you can also make it part of your project management software program and make it collaborative; for example, team members can collaborate on marking milestones or regular reporting of results.

Ask for feedback from your team. Ask them to review the guidelines and let you know if there is anything that's unclear. They may also have ideas at this stage to streamline the process. For example, a sales person who's out there in the field selling may feel that a sales goal is unrealistic and suggest something more reasonable.

Best Practices for Keeping Your Team Focused

As mentioned above, involve your team in the creation and implementation of your plan. If your team members have a hand in creating and implementing the action steps, they'll be more engaged and more in-tune with what you're doing.

- ❏ **Try to be as concise as possible.** Give your team members all the details and the big-picture view, but you don't want to overwhelm them with overly complex guidelines. Pare it down to the necessities and focus on concision and clarity.

- ❏ **Maintain two-way communication.** In addition to asking for feedback from your team members, keep in contact with them throughout the project and make sure they know they can talk to you if they have problems, questions, or concerns. One way to do this is through regular one-on-one coaching.

❑ **Create and maintain strong relationships** with your team members and between your team members. People who know each other will work together better, and this eases any kind of communication. If you know your team members well, you'll understand their way of working, know how they communicate, can give feedback effectively, and so on.

❑ **Make sure you've delegated** the right tasks to the right team members. If someone is bogged down doing something they're not qualified to do, or if they're struggling in some other way, it will be nearly impossible for them to stay focused.

❑ **Standardize practices with solid protocols.** Create business protocols for getting the work done that are routine and consistent to help people stay on the same page.

❑ **Make sure that you're focused, yourself!** As a team leader, you set an example for your team, so you need to make sure that you're clear and focused on your goals and strategies first. Make sure you understand the plan you've created thoroughly.

❑ **Organize your team with to-do lists.** A to-do list offers a focused, prioritized list of specific actions that need to be done. If you can provide to-do lists to your team and each member, this helps everyone stay on task and understand priorities.

❑ **Look for inefficiencies**. Go over your action plan and protocols and look for ways you can save time and work for your team members. When people get bogged down with routine tasks that could be carried out more efficiently, they'll lose focus and burn out.

❑ **Create a schedule and rhythm.** Create a workflow that is the same or similar each day so your team members know what to expect. For example, hold a regular meeting in the morning at the same time, with coaching sessions scheduled throughout the day. If a team member knows that they have two hours to work in the morning, they can be their most focused during that time.

❑ **Motivate your team.** Give them regular reminders of the goals you're working toward and the reasons for the goals. Create small rewards for each milestone or each achievement, and spread the rewards evenly around so that no one feels unappreciated.

❑ **Deal with conflicts immediately as they arise.** Try to defuse conflicts and resolve them in such a way that all parties are satisfied.

❑ **Let your team members blow off steam.** It's good to run a tight ship but give your team members plenty of opportunities to relax and unwind as well. Small breaks help people maintain focus. Break up the process with lunches, parties, and other social engagements where people can forget about work and just have fun.

Best Practices for Eliminating Distractions for Your Team

You'll also keep your team focused on your goal and the tasks at hand if you eliminate distractions as much as possible. Here are some guidelines for doing that.

❑ **Keep the lines of communication work-focused.** If you're using a project management app, or Slack, or simply a work email, make sure the communications remain focused on the work at hand. Occasional personal messages may be permitted, but try to keep personal chatter to breaks, other communication channels, or other non-work time.

❑ **Create an environment that's conducive to concentration.** It's okay to have fun stuff around the workplace, but remove anything that could be potentially distracting, or remove potential distractions to another part of the office.

❑ **Provide incentives only if they make sense.** It's great to offer rewards and incentives, but don't create an incentive program so complex or so rewarding that your team members are just working for the rewards. Use it to motivate, but don't let it distract from your goals.

❑ **Offer tips for your team members** on managing their personal technology while working. For example, you may recommend to them to turn off all notifications for sites like Facebook or chatting apps. Give them time during the schedule to manage social media or other personal technology.

❑ **Make sure priorities are clear.** Your team members may have routine work to do in addition to work on your project. Help them schedule and prioritize so that they never have to do two things at once.

Action Steps:

❑ Draft your Team Communication Plan to share with all team members involved in your marketing, even if you only have one person involved.

❏ Include the elements listed in your plan. Use either the table in your Action Guide or the separate spreadsheet provided.

- ○ Core values for your business

- ○ Your most profitable products and services

- ○ Description of your best customers and why they buy from you

- ○ The #1 marketing goal for the next 3 months

- ○ The #1 marketing strategy to focus on for the next 3 months

- ○ The top 5 tasks for implementing this strategy

- ○ Each person's role in implementing the strategy, along with due dates.

The Next Steps

Now that you've worked through the course, you're ready to implement your first three-month strategy. You'll finally be able to focus and use the results you get to refine the Rapid Results Marketing Formula for your next three-month goal.

Working through this course, you learned:

❑ The importance of prioritizing and why it's not a good idea to multitask

❑ The key steps involved in creating a Rapid Results Marketing Plan to help you avoid distraction, overwork, and burnout and instead focus so that you achieve the results you desire

❑ How to define the foundation for your project that will deliver the success you seek, including defining your core values and unique value proposition

❑ How to identify the first and foremost priority for your business right now, based on the main challenge you're facing

❑ The way to choose the one marketing strategy that will best overcome those challenges and get you closest to your primary goal

❑ How to discover all the critical elements you need to have in place to efficiently and successfully implement the marketing strategy you've chosen

❑ Key tips and best practices for communicating all of this to your team on an ongoing basis to ensure that they stay focused, motivated, and happy

Now, it's time to review the work you've done and get started.

Action Steps:

Visit www.fireyour.agency/guide to download your Action Guide.

❑ Review the work you did on your Rapid Results Marketing Planner.

❑ List the actions you need to take next to start implementing your plan, such as meeting with key team members to specify detailed tasks, responsibilities and deadlines.

Chapter 10

• • • • • • • • •

Recipes for Business Growth

Congratulations, the fact that you've made it so far tells me that you're serious about taking your business to the next level. Did you know that only 8% of people who buy a nonfiction book actually makes it through the entire book? Out of which, less than 25% of them do implement the insights shared in the book. Which means only 2% of the people who purchase this book will ever take immediate and consistent action.

I want you to be among the 2% of the people whom I call the Mission-Driven entrepreneurs. To help you make the best use of the insights you've learned in this book, I am going to give you something I've never shared with anyone before.

I am on a mission to help 1 million entrepreneurs become better marketers, so they can build better and scale faster. In the past 12 years of running a marketing agency, I've collected, curated and created over 500 marketing playbooks that I call the 'Growth Recipes'. I want to give you a very special *Founding Members Deal* to get your hands on these playbooks that I've spent hundreds of hours curating, testing and implementing for ourselves and our clients.

These Growth Recipes are always evolving and I am adding more to the vault every week.

By following these recipes, anybody can easily implement marketing strategies and growth hacks into their business.

You can also share these with your team to delegate and implement these easy-to-follow checklists and get to rapid results in a very short period of time.

Simply visit GrowthRecipes.com/fya to sign up for the Founding Members Deal. You will be grandfathered into the founder's special pricing for life. We will soon increase the price as we keep adding more content.

In addition to getting instant access to hundreds of checklists, you will also receive access to:

— Weekly mastermind calls on Zoom to learn the industry's best-kept secrets

— **A vibrant community of like-minded entrepreneurs to support each other**

— Exclusive video content for elite members

— **Highly skilled Pre-vetted & Certified *Growth Ambassadors* you can hire to help you implement the Growth Recipes**

— Hundreds of high-performing funnels for you to gain inspiration from

— **Email swipe files for your email marketing sequences**

— Repository of free and paid tools to put your marketing on hyperdrive

— **Free access to quarterly virtual growth summits, and the summit recordings**

— Weekly newsletter of new growth hacks added every week

Here's the link to sign up for a 30-day free access: www.GrowthRecipes.com/fya

Acknowledgements

- With Gratitude -

Writing a book is time consuming and arduous. Without the support of my family and friends, this would have never been possible. I am grateful to my wife, Kirthi, for her constant support and encouragement. Aryan, my son who just celebrated his 2nd birthday, has taught me more than what I have taught him. Much of what I am, is to be attributed to my mother, Vasanthi, who is the sweetest person that I have ever encountered. Thanks is due to my father, KP Gurudas, without whom I would not have been born into this planet. Thank you mom and dad for your continued nourishment and support you've provided me with.

My special thanks to my grandfather, NR Manoharan, and my grandmother, Sasirekha, with whom I was fortunate enough to travel the world and learn how to explore life with utmost curiosity. My grandpa has taught me that I can get whatever I want in my life once I set my mind to it. The time I spent with my grandparents are some of the most cherished memories of my life. I am so grateful for their blessings to keep going forward.

There are some really special friends that I would like to acknowledge here. Ravichandra Bhavanikar and Veeranna Muppayanavarmath, I can't think of a better companionship during the formative years of my life, along with Sanish, Tins,

Mohan and Shakthi - you folks are the longest relationship I've ever had outside of my blood relationship. I can't imagine a life without you all in it.

My superstars, my angels that I had met a few years ago at Awesomeness Fest, who went on to become as close to me as my family - Kamal Seth, Wioleta, Seema Bharwani, Esther Isaiah, Rohit Bagaria, Vikash Kumar, Saranya, Sandarenu, Sulinya, and my amazing friends whom I wish I stayed more in touch with - Mark Duncan, Caroline Grandjean-Thomsen, Paolo Cellini, Clarence Tan, Dee Ferdinand, Donna Cotterel, Azlan, Maverick, Maria, Nitesh, Shobie, Sai Ganeis, Rodolfo Young, Sebastian King, Suchanda, Sunil, Tanya, Terence, Vincent, Laura, Magda, Karlene and so many more beautiful people I met at the AFest.

My super-friends whom I have chose to travel my journey with - Maria Sundar, Beejel and Yoggi Parmar, Akshay and Selvi Cherian, Louiss Lim, Siddharth Rajsekar, Soumitra Paul, Suresh Babu, Gopal Krishnan, Deepak Kanakaraju, Rajiv and Bhakti Sanghavi Talreja, Lokesh and Manasa, Kartika Nair, and a special mention to Jyotsna Ramachandran who coached and mentored me towards completing this book you're holding in your hands.

My NASSCOM and CAFIT friends whom I cherish so much, and continue to inspire me to this day - Duleep Sahadevan, Dr. Saji Gopinath, Charles Thomas, Purushottaman, Ravi Gururaj, Senthil, Sujith Unni, Madhavan Ramakrishnan, Vijith Sivadasan, Ajay Thomas, Jijo Joseph, Harshad, Sainul Abidheen, Gafoor, Haris, Deepak, Kavitha, Bijith, Roshik, Akhil, Vinoop, Amar, Arun, Axel, Asif, Noufal, Nishanth, Anvar, Sajeer, Preethi, Rijas, Suhail, Vinod, Vipin and countless others who made my entrepreneurial journey worth it.

It is an honor to be of service to my hundreds of clients from whom I've learned so much about being a service provider. It is impossible for me to mention everyone here but I want to acknowledge my closest ones that I consider as my greatest friends: Steven Moreland, Roy Meyer, Karl Maier, Dustin Mathews, Pete Rakozy, Arun Varghese, Phillip Milakovich, Andreea Elena Halikia, Kevin Judge, Dr. Norman Deitch, John Castagnini, Tim J Pyle, Heather Walker, Ava Rebekah Rahman, Yvonne Dayan, Mark Green, Jaime Ellen, Lakshman TL of Apollo Hospitals, Antony Marshal, Becky Smith, Hira Syed, and so many more that the list will be endless.

My deepest gratitude to my incredibly awesome mentors - Santosh Nair, Troy Dean, Craig Jacobson, Christopher Friend, Errol Abramson (Canada's Billionaire Business Tycoon), AJ Mirabedini, Evan Carmichael, Jared Codling, Parthiv and Dipa Shah, Henry Kaminsky, Kellsie Moore, Austin Netzley, Brain Downard, Elissa Weinzimmer, Kevin Barber, Dan Tyre, Luke Summerfeild, Manoj Chugani, Amanda Holmes, Dr. Philip Agrios, Kelly O'Neil, Scott Oldford, Sam Ovens, Rajiv Parikh and Vinod Nambiar (My ex-bosses at Position2), Janak Mehta, Katya Sarmiento, Lior Ohayon, Troy Broussard, Adam Franklin, and several others whom I was lucky to cross paths with.

Special thanks to my dear ex-colleagues at WebNamaste (too long a list to mention but they are always in my heart) and my existing core team members Ashna Baby, Athira, Rakesh, Jaseel, and my strategic partner Shivani Gupta who is also my longtime friend from college. My sincere gratitude to the leaders at WebNamaste that I was fortunate to work with - Rajeev Cyril, Rakesh T Nair, Praveena Manoj, Zainu, Haris Karat and Shyam Sundar. A special shoutout to Rituja Upadhyay - my mentee and a shining example of a lifelong learner.

Expressing my gratitude and appreciation to Shaheer of Greater Design Co. for the amazing branding and artwork on our projects and our client projects.

Sending healing wishes and prayers to Hemal Makhija, my book launch buddy who is battling with cancer.

Finally my publishing team at NotionPress, who have been an absolute pleasure to work with.